ColdFusion XML Objects

Jeff Peters

Proton Arts – Manassas VA USA

ColdFusion XML Objects
Copyright © 2006 by Proton Arts
FIRST EDITION: March 2006

0009 08 07 06 7 6 5 4 3 2 1

ISBN 0-9752647-5-3

Interpretation of the printing code: The rightmost double-digit number is the year of the book's publication; the rightmost single-digit number is the number of the book's publication. For example, the printing code 04-1 shows that the first publication of the book occurred in 2004.
Published in the United States of America

Trademarks

All terms mentioned in this book that known to be trademarks or service marks have been appropriately capitalized. Proton Arts cannot attest to the accuracy of this information. Use of a term in this book should not be regarded as affecting the validity of any trademark or service mark. ColdFusion, is a registered trademarks of Adobe, Inc. Fusebox is a registered trademark of Fusebox, Inc. BlueDragon is a trademark of New Atlanta Communications. Firefox is a registered trademark of The Mozilla Foundation. The Simpsons is a registered trademark of Matt Groening.

Warning and Disclaimer

This book is designed to provide information about ColdFusion programming. Every effort has been made to make this book as complete with respect to its topic and as accurate as possible, but no warranty of fitness is implied.
The information is provided on an as-is basis. The author and Proton Arts shall have neither liability nor responsibility to any person or entity with respect to any loss or damages arising from the information contained in this book or from the use of the programs that may accompany it.

This book was written and set with OpenOffice.org 2.0

Dedication

For Daddy

You realize you're one of the ones responsible for getting me into this whole mess, don't you?

About the Author

Jeff Peters is a project manager and application architect for Operational Technologies Services, Inc. Jeff has been involved in information systems in one way or another since 1973, when he first crash-landed a lunar module on a teletype terminal to the Dartmouth University mainframe. That same machine predicted that he would one day become either a shepherd or President of the United States. Neither of these predictions seems to have been fulfilled.

Involved in the Internet since the late '80s, Jeff was unfortunately working on mainframe projects (taking a hiatus from LAN-based systems) when the 'Net went public and changed the face of application delivery forever. Some days he thinks he still hasn't caught up, but he's found that writing books is a good way to keep in practice. Jeff co-wrote *Fusebox: Developing ColdFusion Applications* (New Riders, 2002) and authored *ColdFusion Lists, Arrays, and Structures* (Proton Arts, 2004), *Fusebox 4 and FLiP: Master-Class ColdFusion Applications* (Proton Arts, 2004), *What's New in Fusebox 4.1, The Fusebox Guidebook,* and *The Collected Webspinner* (Proton Arts, 2005). He has also contributed to publications such as *ColdFusion Developer's Journal*, *Capital PC Monitor*, and *PocketPC Magazine*. His web-development-oriented web site, GrokFusebox.com, provides a gateway to a wide variety of resources, and his podcast with Hal Helms, "Helms and Peters Out Loud", is heard weekly at www.helmsandpeters.com . Jeff can be reached at jeff@grokfusebox.com.

Acknowledgments

I would like to acknowledge Tom Hopkins and Operational Technologies Services, Inc. For over a decade now they have been supporting and encouraging my efforts in the writing, speaking, and training world. Thanks, Tom.

Jeff Peters
March, 2006

Table of Contents

Chapter 1 - Introduction to XML

XML has become a very prevalent technology in recent years. Unfortunately, though many people in the tech sector talk about XML quite a bit, many also have very little understanding of what XML is and how to use it. For us ColdFusion developers, taking on the task of learning XML can be a bit daunting. There is a large variety of thousand-page tomes on the XML specification and its uses in information technology.

The problem, it seems to me, is that XML is too big a subject to address as a monolith. There are so many potential applications for XML that generalist reference works become cumbersome to read and understand. With that in mind, this book addresses XML from one specific perspective: that of the ColdFusion developer.

Like other books in this series from Proton Arts, *ColdFusion XML Objects* is a short, concise discussion. We'll look at creating, updating, and manipulating XML objects in ColdFusion. As part of those activities, we'll look at topics like XPath and XSLT. But this is by no means an exhaustive reference on those subjects. This book is designed to be the one you reach for first, not the one with all the answers to every question on XML.

Before we get into the nuts and bolts of manipulating XML objects, we'll take a brief look at the history of XML. It's hard to talk comfortably about a topic without some basic understanding of the background. If you already have the basics, and need to address a specific issue with XML in ColdFusion, feel free to skip the rest of this chapter. There won't be a test at the end--I promise.

A Little History

XML (eXtensible Markup Language) has been variously called a subset of Standard Generalized Markup Language (SGML), an offshoot of SGML, or an attempt to subvert SGML. Regardless of the commentator's opinion, XML has its roots in SGML.

SGML is a markup (i.e., tag-based) language that has been used for many years, particularly to document large-scale projects. One of the largest proponents of SGML has been Boeing, which uses the language to document aircraft designs.

When the World Wide Web Consortium (W3C) decided to create a language to define content (as opposed to HTML, which combines content and presentation), they used SGML as a model on which to base XML. XML was to be a new markup language that would allow the user to define the tags to be used. That is, the language would be extensible.

The point behind XML is to define and transmit data. In this respect, I often refer to it as the reason ASCII was created--it just took us 30 or so years to figure that out.

ASCII, Commas and Columns

The American Standard Code for Information Interchange (ASCII) is the character encoding system that carried personal computing and other systems through the 1980s. (Though still a valid standard, ASCII has been supplanted in recent years by an ANSI standard that is somewhat more international in nature.) ASCII is simply a definition for translating binary data into human-readable characters.

For years, ASCII text files have been used to transfer data between systems. Until the advent of XML, this was done through two predominant methods: fixed-width column format and comma-delimited (aka comma-separated values or CSV) format. Both of these format represent a record of data as one line in the file.

Fixed-width column format, as its name indicates, uses a column of a predetermined width for each data field. For example, we might see a dataset that look like this:

```
Last         First        Age Role
Simpson      Homer        41  father
Simpson      Marge        39  mother
Simpson      Bart         10  son
Simpson      Lisa          8  daughter
Simpson      Maggie        1  daughter
Simpson      Grandpa      72  grandfather
```

This is a workable dataset, though it has its drawbacks. For example, if anything causes a misalignment in a column, the data gets corrupted. Worse, an automated import routine wouldn't know that the data is corrupted, as it simply reads whatever is (or isn't) in the specified columns. So if the first letter of Bart's record were somehow deleted, his name would be read as **`art impson`** and his role would be **`on`**, due to the column shifts.

The fragility of fixed-width data led to the creation of comma-delimited format, which uses commas to separate the data in each field, and quotes to qualify strings (this allows commas to actually be used in field values). Our Simpsons example in comma-delimited format would look like this:

```
"Last","First","Age","Role"
"Simpson","Homer",41,"father"
"Simpson","Marge",39,"mother"
"Simpson","Bart",10,"son"
"Simpson","Lisa",8,"daughter"
"Simpson","Maggie",1,"daughter"
"Simpson","Grandpa",72,"grandfather"
```

Comma-delimited formats are a little less fragile than fixed-width formats. If the 'S' was dropped from Bart's last name in the second example, the only field that would have incorrect data would be his last name. On the other hand, if the quote were left off the beginning of the line, the dataset wouldn't import correctly.

Then, along came the Web. Data communication exploded all over the world. People everywhere began to publish data on the web in HTML. Data analysts soon realized that HTML, while very useful, presents a big problem: it combines content and presentation, a fundamental no-no in terms of efficient data management. So came the impetus for the W3C to create XML.

XML uses tags to define fields in a dataset. In so doing, the data becomes self-documenting, and very robust. Because of the rules that define the use of XML, we can easily test to see that an XML set is written according to the rules (i.e., is well-formed), and conforms to a specific use (i.e., is valid). We'll visit the topics of well-formedness and validity a bit more in the next section. For now, let's look at our Simpsons data defined as XML:

```
<people>
  <person lastName="Simpson" firstName="Homer" age="41" role="father" />
  <person lastName="Simpson" firstName="Marge" age="39" role="mother" />
  <person lastName="Simpson" firstName="Bart" age="10" role="son" />
  <person lastName="Simpson" firstName="Lisa" age="8" role="daughter" />
  <person lastName="Simpson" firstName="Maggie" age="1" role="daughter" />
  <person lastName="Simpson" firstName="Grandpa" age="72" role="grandfather" />
</people>
```

One of the key characteristics of XML is that the definition of a given dataset is left up to the party that is responsible for the data. Data can be encoded using elements with attributes, as shown above, or as elements alone, with data describing characteristics of an element treated as child elements instead of attributes. Consequently, we could just as well have defined our Simpsons XML dataset to look like this:

```
<people>
  <person>
    <lastName>Simpson</lastName>
    <firstName>Homer</firstName>
    <age>41</age>
    <role>father</role>
  </person>
  <person>
    <lastName>Simpson</lastName>
    <firstName>Marge</firstName>
    <age>39</age>
    <role>mother</role>
  </person>
  <person>
    <lastName>Simpson</lastName>
    <firstName>Bart</firstName>
    <age>10</age>
    <role>son</role>
  </person>
  <person>
    <lastName>Simpson</lastName>
    <firstName>Lisa</firstName>
    <age>8</age>
    <role>daughter</role>
  </person>
  <person>
    <lastName>Simpson</lastName>
    <firstName>Maggie</firstName>
    <age>1</age>
    <role>daughter</role>
  </person>
  <person>
    <lastName>Simpson</lastName>
    <firstName>Grandpa</firstName>
    <age>72</age>
    <role>grandfather</role>
  </person>
</people>
```

The last two examples use two different XML defintions, or vocabularies, to define the same data. In order to discuss the differences and reasons for them, we need to pick up a little jargon.

Some Terminology

Tags in XML are referred to as elements. If an element has values encoded within its start tag (like in the first Simpsons example above), they are called attributes. An attribute has a name (to the left of the equals sign) and a value (to the right).

When parsing XML with XPath, elements are also referred to as nodes. The first element in an XML set is called the root element or root node.

A set of definitions for using XML in a particular application is called a vocabulary. Vocabularies are defined using a Document Type Definition or an XML schema.

An XML dataset that follows the basic rules of writing XML is said to be well-formed. An XML set that is well-formed and follows a particular vocabulary is said to be valid.

With the basic terms in hand and a couple of examples behind us, we can look at the basic rules for writing an XML dataset.

Basic Rules

As stated in the last section, in order for an XML dataset to be well-formed, it must follow the basic rules of XML syntax. This section details the basic rules, condensed from the the World Wide Web Consortium's recommendation for XML, Third Edition.

NOTE: The complete XML recommendation can be found at http://www.w3.org/TR/REC-xml/

Basic Rule 1. The dataset contains one or more elements.

This rule is a bit obvious, but it is important. Let's assume we use an automated process to create an XML dataset, then subject that dataset to a transformation (we'll work with transformations at length later). For some reason, we encounter a condition that causes an empty dataset to be produced by the first part of our process. When we subject the dataset to transformation, we'll get an error (as opposed to an empty output, as some might expect).

Basic Rule 2. There is exactly one root element.

The first element that occurs in an XML dataset is called the root element. There can be only one root element. For example, the following dataset is well-formed:

```
<lunchbox>
  <item>Peanut butter and jelly sandwich</item>
  <item>Carrot sticks</item>
</lunchbox>
```

but this second dataset is not:

```
<item>Peanut butter and jelly sandwich</item>
<item>Carrot sticks</item>
```

Where the first example has a single root node (`<lunchbox>`), the second dataset has two `<item>` nodes competing for the root node spot. Similarly, the following dataset is not well-formed:

```
<entree>Peanut butter and jelly sandwich</entree>
<drink>Carrot sticks</drink>
```

Even though the two nodes have different names, they exist at the same level in the XML hierarchy. Consequently, they compete for the root node spot (actually, in both of the previous two examples the first element is the root node; the second is an error).

Basic Rule 3. Non-root elements nest properly.

Each element's start-tag and end-tag must exist within the same parent element. The only element that has no parent is the root element. One of the most common examples of this is in the difference between HTML and XHTML (which is an XML vocabulary). The following example is valid HTML, but is not well-formed XHTML:

```
<b><i>ColdFusion XML Objects</b></i>
```

In order for the example to be well-formed, the tags must be properly nested:

```
<b><i>ColdFusion XML Objects</i></b>
```

Proper nesting is easier to see if we add some carriage returns to the examples:

```
<b>
  <i>
   ColdFusion XML Objects
</b>
  </i>
```

looks ugly and broken, whereas

```
<b>
  <i>
   ColdFusion XML Objects
  </i>
</b>
```

looks neat and balanced. XML is nothing if not neat and balanced.

Basic Rule 4. Elements have either a start-tag and an end-tag, or are empty elements.

This rule is sometimes stated as, "All elements must have an ending." The two ways to end an element are with an end-tag or as an empty element. Start and end tags are readily recognized:

```
<person></person>
```

An empty element is simply an element that has only one tag. So instead of a start-tag and an end-tag, there's only one tag to indicate the entire element. An empty element has a slash preceding the right angle-bracket at the end of the tag. For example, the `<br>` tag from HTML becomes `<br />` in XHTML.

Empty elements may have attributes, but they cannot have child elements, for the simple reason that there's no end tag to enclose children. Our first Simpsons example uses an empty element for each person:

```
<person lastName="Simpson" firstName="Homer" age="41" role="father" />
```

Regardless of whether we use tag pairs or empty elements, we need to make sure each element is properly closed. Watch those ending slashes in empty elements--they are easily overlooked.

Basic Rule 5. Attribute values are delimited by quotes.

In XML, all attribute values must have a quote character preceding and following the value. This is strict territory for HTML coders, who are accustomed to the optional nature of delimiters for attribute values in HTML. This example is valid HTML, but not valid XHTML:

```
<body bgcolor=#FFAA0C></body>
```

The well-formed equivalent looks like this:

```
<body bgcolor="#FFAA0C"></body>
```

As with the trailing slashes on empty elements, the delimiting quotes on attribute values are easy to forget when creating XML data by hand (or templates that will generate XML).

Basic Rule 6. No attribute is repeated in an element.

An XML dataset that has two instances of the same attribute within an element is not well-formed. Again we can look to HTML for common examples. The following example will work in an HTML browser:

```
<body bgcolor="#00FF00" bgcolor="#FF0000"></body>
```

The browser will use the first instance and ignore the second. However, this is not well-formed XML (and therefore not well-formed XHTML).

Basic Rule 7. Elements and attributes are case-sensitive.

This is an easy rule to overlook when debugging problems with XML data, particularly for those of us who don't have a great deal of experience with case-sensitive languages or operating systems. Simply put, the case of letters in XML must match. Here is an example of a violation of this rule that will cause an error:

```
<person>Fred</Person>
```

And here's a more subtle variation on the theme:

```
<person>Fred</person>
<Person>Ethel</Person>
```

This last example is well-formed (assuming Fred and Ethel are contained by an unspecified parent), but it is guaranteed to cause hair loss when run, because one of the two will be properly processed while the other will be ignored (depending on whether **person** or **Person** is the correct element name).

OK, that about does it for the basics of creating well-formed XML. We've looked at some history, and we know how to build the stuff--at least enough to get started. That leaves us with just one pivotal question: What's this XML stuff good for anyway?

Some Uses for XML

XML is becoming a pervasive standard in the world of the web. Everywhere you turn there's more XML popping up. Typically, it hides pretty well, not making a big deal of itself, often masquerading under another acronym altogether.

In the ColdFusion world, we've been using XML for years without even caring that it's XML. This is on account of the Web Distributed Data eXchange (WDDX) standard. WDDX is an XML vocabulary designed for exchanging data between web-based environments, most commonly ColdFusion and Javascript.

Many CFers are also Fuseboxers, and Fusebox 4 brings XML into the game with its application and circuit configuration files, both of which use XML vocabularies; and Fusedoc 2.0, another XML vocabulary.

If we deal with web services, we deal with XML, though probably not directly. The Web Services Description Language (WSDL) is an XML vocabulary, as is the Simple Object Access Protocol (SOAP).

We are increasingly surrounded by datasets defined as XML. This is a good thing, since once we know how to deal with XML and have a common toolset available, we can deal with any of the new vocabularies that pop up.

Let's Get Going

We've taken a look at the history of XML, how to put it together, some terminology, the basic rules, and some common uses. Now we're ready to get to the fun stuff--the actual tinkering with XML in ColdFusion. We'll look at how to create XML objects, how to work with data contained within XML objects, and how to get output from (transform) XML data. It should be a lot of fun.

Chapter 2 - XML Objects in CFML

When we manipulate XML datasets in CFML, we use a special datatype called an *XML object*. XML objects allow us direct handling of XML-based data, rather than being forced to manipulate the XML itself. This is a rather subtle distinction, but hopefully it will become clearer as we go along.

XML objects in CFML resemble structures. The syntax used to reference data in an XML object is similar to the dot notation used to reference data in a structure. Let's start by looking at our Simpsons example from Chapter 1 through the lens of the `<cfdump>` tag:

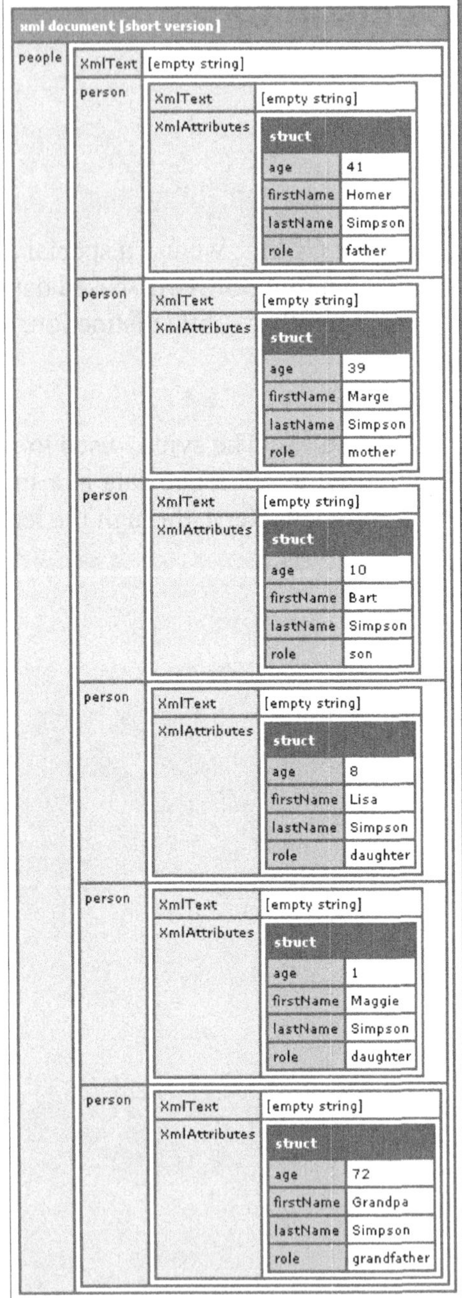

Illustration 1: XML Object <cfdump>

You might have already noticed that the dump in Illustration 1 contains several items labeled XmlAttributes. We are using the example from Chapter 1 that stores person information with attributes as well as elements. We'll stick with this version so we can look at attribute-oriented issues as well as those for elements.

Referring to Data in an XML Object

Like a structure, we can refer to data in an XML object using dotted notation. For example, we can use the notation myFamily.people.person[1].firstName to find out the firstName of the first person: **Homer**. (The XML object we're working with is named myFamily.)

This notation looks somewhat like structure notation, but there's a bracketed index number in the middle, too, like typical array notation. When there are multiple occurrences of an element in an XML object, they can be referenced like an array. The six person elements in the myFamily XML object are indexed 1-6.

Based on this knowledge, we could get right to work using the data in this XML object by using typical ColdFusion code. For example, if we wanted to list out all the firstNames in the myFamily variable, we could use the following code:

```
<cfoutput>
  <cfloop from="1" to="#ArrayLen(myFamily.people.person)#" index="i">
    #myFamily.people.person[i].XmlAttributes["firstName"]#<br>
  </cfloop>
</cfoutput>
```

CFMX vs. BlueDragon:
BlueDragon also allows the following, more simplified syntax:

```
<cfoutput>
  <cfloop from="1" to="#ArrayLen(myFamily.people.person)#" index="i">
    #myFamily.people.person[i].firstName#<br>
  </cfloop>
</cfoutput>
```

This will cause an error in CFMX.

This bit of code works perfectly well, but it overlooks the real power of XML. While it is important to recognize that ColdFusion makes it very easy to import and manipulate XML data with familiar CFML code, it is also very important to understand the immense opportunities that are presented by the ability to manipulate an XML object using XML-specific techniques. These techniques include extracting data with XPath and transforming data with XSL stylesheets. These techniques will be discussed in later chapters.

Before we move on to advanced data manipulation using XML objects, let's take some time to look at some properties of XML objects in CFML.

CFML XML Object Properties

Every XML object in CFML has a set of properties that expose information about the object. Similarly, each element (node) in the object has its own set of properties. The following sections discuss each property in the context of our Simpsons example.

An XML object has properties called XmlRoot and XmlComment. These properties are not displayed as part of the XML object if we view it with `<cfdump>` but they are displayed in debug output. They must be referenced explicitly. In addition to these two properties, each element within an XML object has several more properties, including XmlAttributes, XmlCData, XmlChildren, XmlName, XmlText, and XmlValue.

The following pages discuss each of these properties. For each property, we'll see what data it returns, and whether or not it may exist for a given XML object.

XmlRoot Property

The XmlRoot property always exists for an XML object. This property returns the content of the XML object contained within the root node. In the case of our Simpsons example, `<cfdump var="#myFamily.XmlRoot#">` returns the following:

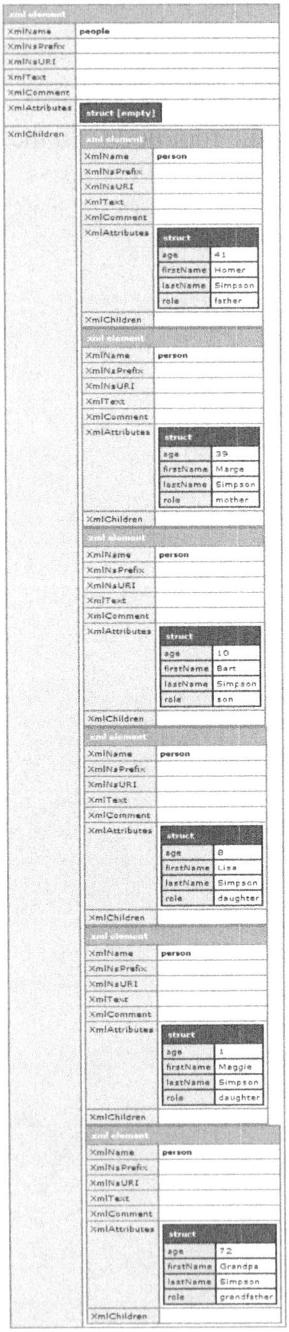

Illustration 2: XmlRoot for Simpsons Example

XmlComment Property

The XmlComment property returns any comments made at the top of the XML data that was used to create the XML object. A comment may or may not exist, depending on the source XML and the method used to create the XML object.

In our Simpsons example, there is no comment in the XML data, so the XmlComment property returns an empty string. Let's take a look at an XML dataset that would result in an XML object with something in its XMLComment property.

```
<cfxml variable="myVehicle">
  <!-- This dataset contains a car. -->
  <car>
    <doors count="2" />
    <wheels count="4" />
  </car>
</cfxml>
```

If we now request #myVehicle.XMLComment#, we'll get back the string **This dataset contains a car**.

The XMLComment property collects any comments that are not contained within the node structure of the XML dataset. So, if we changed the example above to look like this:

```
<cfxml variable="myVehicle">
  <!-- This dataset contains a car. -->
  <car>
    <!-- It's a sports car -->
    <doors count="2" />
    <wheels count="4" />
  </car>
  <!-- And no trucks. -->
</cfxml>
```

And once again request #myVehicle.XMLComment#, we'll get back the string **This dataset contains a car. And no trucks.** The comment within the dataset's elements (<!-- It's a sports car -->) is not part of the XML object's XMLComment. It is, however, part of the <car> element's XMLComment. So, if we requested #myVehicle.car.XmlComment#, we would get **It's a sports car**.

XmlDocType Property

The XmlDocType property returns information based on the existence of a DOCTYPE tag at the beginning of the XML data. If no doctype tag is included, calling the XmlDocType property results in an error for both CFMX and BlueDragon.

This doctype definition at the beginning of an XHTML dataset:

```
<!DOCTYPE html PUBLIC "-//W3C//DTD XHTML 1.0 Transitional//EN"
"http://www.w3.org/TR/xhtml1/DTD/xhtml1-transitional.dtd">
```

would result in the following <cfdump> output:

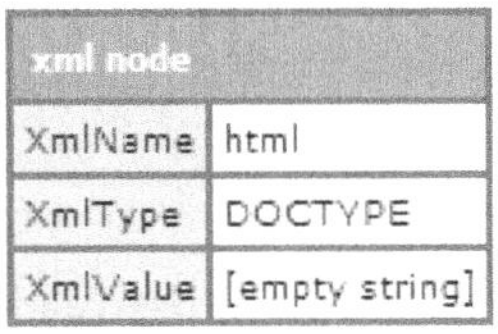

xml node	
XmlName	html
XmlType	DOCTYPE
XmlValue	[empty string]

Illustration 3: XmlDoctype <cfdump>

In most cases when dealing with XML within applications, we won't have to worry about extracting DocType data. There's really not much purpose in doing so, since the DocType exists to provide the XML with a source for validation. If the XML dataset passes that validation, we generally don't need to know much more with respect to the DocType. The point of this section is simply to let you know that the XmlDocType property exists.

So now we can extract some information about the XML object itself. We are ready to move on and look at the properties of the elements within the XML object.

ColdFusion XML Object Element Properties

Just as an XML object has properties, each element within an XML object has properties of its own. They are named XmlText, XmlCData, XmlChildren, XmlName, XmlComment, XmlValue, and XmlAttributes. They are all string values, except for XmlChildren (an array) and XmlAttributes (a structure). These properties always exist for a given element, though they may be empty. This means that we can reference any of these variables without fear of throwing an error. We only need to test for the value of the variable, instead of testing for existence first.

The following pages discuss each of these properties. For each property, we'll see what data it returns, and whether or not it may exist for a given XML object.

XmlText Property

The XmlText property returns any text that is contained inside the specified element, outside its child nodes, and ignoring any comments.

Let's add a bit of text to the <people> element of the Simpsons example and see what happens:

```
<cfxml variable="myFamily">
  <people>This is the Simpson family. <!-- We want this text to show -->
    <person lastName="Simpson" firstName="Homer" age="41" role="father" />
    <person lastName="Simpson" firstName="Marge" age="39" role="mother" />
    <person lastName="Simpson" firstName="Bart" age="10" role="son" />
    <person lastName="Simpson" firstName="Lisa" age="8" role="daughter" />
    <person lastName="Simpson" firstName="Maggie" age="1" role="daughter" />
    <person lastName="Simpson" firstName="Grandpa" age="72" role="grandfather" />
  </people>
</cfxml>
```

Now if we output `#myFamily.people.XmlText#`, we get this result:

```
This is the Simpson family.
```

The comment is not included in the XmlText property. Only non-comment text and CDATA sections are included in the XmlText property. What's a CDATA section? Let's take a look.

CDATA Sections

Like other tag-based markup languages, XML restricts the characters that are allowed to appear inside a tag pair. We can't use `<` or `&` in XML, and it's a good idea to also avoid `>`, `'`, and `"`. These characters can be replaced by entity references, just as we do with HTML:

<, &, >, ', and ".

However, we sometimes need to be able to include text with these special characters within an XML dataset. This is where CDATA comes in. A CDATA section is just a section of text enclosed inside a special tag so that the illegal characters can be used. CDATA sections are often used when we need include a section of code in the data without encoding it.

Let's add a CDATA section to the example and see how it affects the XmlText property:

```
<cfxml variable="myFamily">
 <people>This is the Simpson family. <!-- We want this text to show -->
  <![CDATA[Hopefully Bart knows that 1 < 2 and 3 > 0, but I don't know for sure.]]>
  <person lastName="Simpson" firstName="Homer" age="41" role="father" />
  <person lastName="Simpson" firstName="Marge" age="39" role="mother" />
  <person lastName="Simpson" firstName="Bart" age="10" role="son" />
  <person lastName="Simpson" firstName="Lisa" age="8" role="daughter" />
  <person lastName="Simpson" firstName="Maggie" age="1" role="daughter" />
  <person lastName="Simpson" firstName="Grandpa" age="72" role="grandfather" />
 </people>
</cfxml>
```

Now when we reference #myFamily.people.XmlText#, the result is

```
This is the Simpson family. Hopefully Bart knows that 1 < 2
and 3 > 0, but I don't know for sure.
```

So the XmlText property pulled out the content in the CDATA section. That is, everything between the starting markup <![CDATA[and the ending markup]]>. This content is include in the XmlText property for the <people> element.

Having discussed CDATA in the context of the XmlText property, we can now look at another property: XmlCData.

XmlCData Property

The XmlCData property behaves somewhat differently than we might expect. It would be logical to think that, where XmlText returns all the non-comment text within an element, XmlCData returns only the CDATA content, if any exists.

This, however, is not the case. In truth, the XmlCData property is essentially a synonym for the XmlText property. If we look back at the examples we used above for the XmlText property, requesting `#myFamily.XmlText#` or `#myFamily.XmlCData#` results in exactly the same output.

XmlChildren Property

The XmlChildren property is an array that contains all elements that are children of the specified element. In our Simpsons example, all the `<person>` elements are children of the `<people>` element. Consequently, if we use `<cfdump var="#myFamily.people.XmlChildren#">`, the result is the array shown in Illustration 4.(The illustration has been rearranged to fit on one page.)

As the illustration shows, `myFamily.people.XmlChildren` holds an array of all the child elements of the `myFamily.people` element. But what happens if the children have child elements of their own? Are they included in the XmlChildren property of the original parent (i.e., the "grandparent" of the lowest level)? Let's find out.

We'll modify the basic Simpsons example so Bart has a pet:

```
<people>
  <person lastName="Simpson" firstName="Homer" age="41" role="father" />
  <person lastName="Simpson" firstName="Marge" age="39" role="mother" />
  <person lastName="Simpson" firstName="Bart" age="10" role="son">
    <pet name="Santa's Little Helper" />
  </person>
  <person lastName="Simpson" firstName="Lisa" age="8" role="daughter" />
  <person lastName="Simpson" firstName="Maggie" age="1" role="daughter" />
  <person lastName="Simpson" firstName="Grandpa" age="72" role="grandfather" />
</people>
```

Now if we use `<cfdump var="#myFamily.people.XmlChildren#">`, the result is the array shown in Illustration 5. Note that the array member for Bart does indeed contain the new child element.

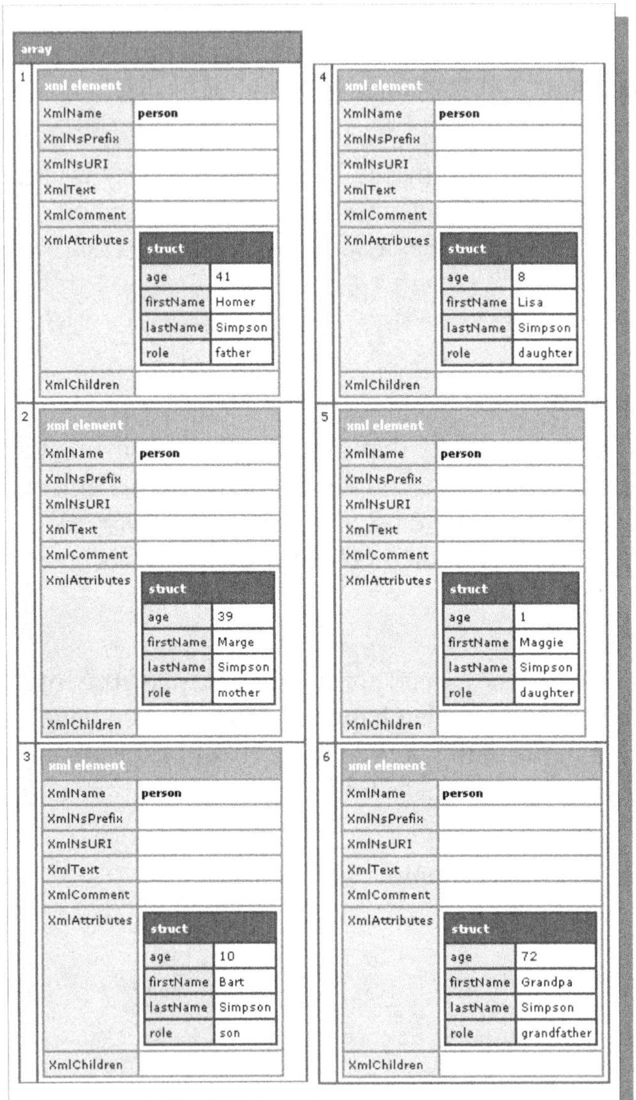

Illustration 4: XmlChildren Array

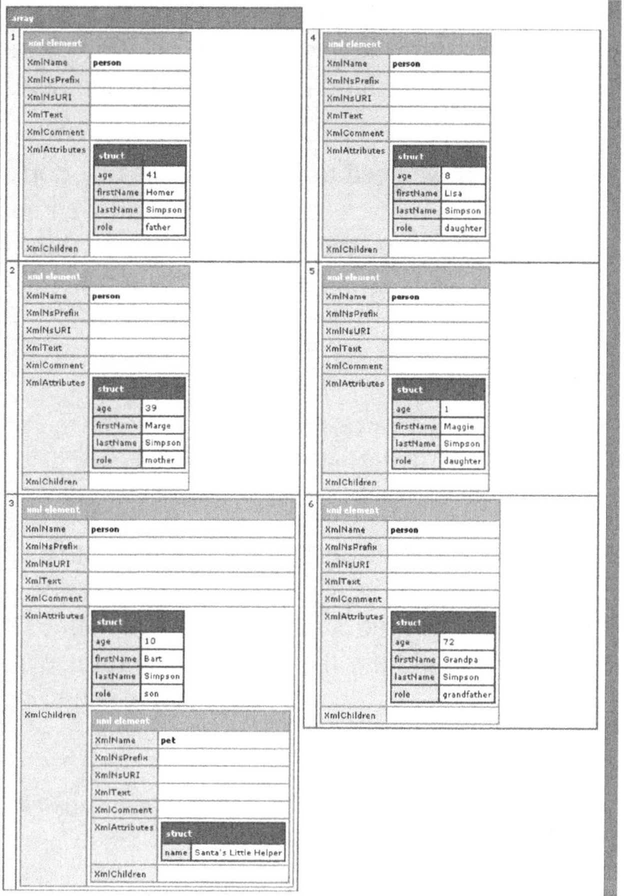

Illustration 5: XmlChildren Take 2

Of course, we can treat the XmlChildren array just like any other ColdFusion array in terms of code. For example, if we wanted to get the firstName of each person in the family, we could use this code:

```
<cfloop from="1" to="#ArrayLen(myFamily.people.XmlChildren)#" index="i">
  <cfoutput>#myFamily.people.XmlChildren[i].XmlAttributes.firstName#</cfoutput><br>
</cfloop>
```

So there's nothing really mysterious about the XmlChildren property. If we know how to manipulate ColdFusion arrays, we know how to manipulate the data this property returns.[1]

1 Arrays are covered in depth in my book *ColdFusion Lists, Arrays, & Structures*, from Proton Arts.

XmlName Property

The XmlName property simply returns the name of the specified element. An element's name is the first word that appears after the **<** character in the element's opening tag.

This property can be very useful if we need to write routines that don't know the XML vocabulary of the object being used. For example, let's say all we know is that we have an XML object variable named **`myFamily`**. We need to know two things: the name of the root node of the object, and how many children it has. The following code answers these two questions.

```
<cfoutput>
The root element is: #myFamily.XmlRoot.XmlName#<br>
It has #ArrayLen(myFamily[myFamily.XmlRoot.XmlName].XmlChildren)# children.
</cfoutput>
```

Where might something like this come in handy? We could create a routine that reads an XML object and turns it into an SQL INSERT statement. If we know the table name is the same as the root node name, and the children are records with values stored as attributes (like our Simpsons example), we could use the this code to produce a set of SQL statements:

```
<cfset rootName = myXMLData.XmlRoot.XmlName>
<cfset childCount = ArrayLen(myXMLData[myXmlData.XmlRoot.XmlName].XmlChildren)>
<cfloop from="1" to="#childCount#" index="i">
  <cfset lstFieldNames = "">
  <cfset lstValues = "">
  <cfloop collection="#myXMLData[rootName].XmlChildren[i].XmlAttributes#" item="thisElement">
    <cfset lstFieldNames = ListAppend(lstFieldNames,thisElement)>
    <cfset lstValues = ListAppend(lstValues,"'#myXMLData[rootName].XmlChildren[i].XmlAttributes
[thisElement]#'")>
  </cfloop>
  <cfoutput>
    INSERT INTO #myXMLData.XmlRoot.XmlName# (#lstFieldNames#) VALUES (#lstValues#)<br>
  </cfoutput>
</cfloop>
```

The preceding code, when applied to our Simpsons example (i.e., saving the `myFamily` variable to `myXmlData` instead), produces this output:

```
INSERT INTO people (lastName,firstName,age,role) VALUES
('Simpson','Homer','41','father')
INSERT INTO people (lastName,firstName,age,role) VALUES
('Simpson','Marge','39','mother')
INSERT INTO people (lastName,firstName,age,role) VALUES
('Simpson','Bart','10','son')
INSERT INTO people (lastName,firstName,age,role) VALUES
('Simpson','Lisa','8','daughter')
INSERT INTO people (lastName,firstName,age,role) VALUES
('Simpson','Maggie','1','daughter')
INSERT INTO people (lastName,firstName,age,role) VALUES
('Simpson','Grandpa','72','grandfather')
```

But the power of the code really becomes apparent when we take another, completely unrelated, XML dataset and process it with the same code. Here's another chunk of CFML to create the myXMLData XML object:

```
<vehicles>
  <vehicle type="truck" VIN="1W1235123512341" make="Dodge" model="Dakota" year="2004" />
  <vehicle type="car" VIN="1X987896127641212" make="Ford" model="Mustang" year="1965" />
  <vehicle type="car" VIN="None" make="Stutz" model="Bearcat" year="1914" />
</vehicles>
```

Running the same piece of code from the first example on this new XML object results in this output:

```
INSERT INTO vehicles (type,VIN,make,model,year) VALUES
('truck','1W1235123512341','Dodge','Dakota','2004')
INSERT INTO vehicles (type,VIN,make,model,year) VALUES
('car','1X987896127641212','Ford','Mustang','1965')
INSERT INTO vehicles (type,VIN,make,model,year) VALUES
('car','None','Stutz','Bearcat','1914')
```

So we can create code to operate on XML objects even if we don't know the exact structure of the object to be processed. We're starting to see some of the power of XML.

NOTE: The same result shown above could be achieved by using an XSL stylesheet to transform the XML data. However, stylesheets are vocabulary-specific, so we would need a different stylesheet for the second example. We'll take a closer look at XSLT later in the book.

XmlComment Property

The XmlComment property returns any comments that are contained by the referenced element. If the element contains more than one comment, the comments are concatenated together without the comment markup.

Let's go back to the vehicle example we used for the XML object's XmlComment property, only this time we'll dump the XmlComment property for the <car> element:

```
<cfxml variable="myVehicle">
 <!-- This dataset contains a car. -->
 <car>
  <!-- It's a sports car. -->
  <doors count="2" />
  <wheels count="4" />
  <!-- This is the end of the car element. -->
 </car>
 <!-- And no trucks. -->
</cfxml>

<cfdump var="#myVehicle.car.XmlComment#">
```

The output in this case is **`It's a sports car. This is the end of the car element.`** The comment markup has been removed, and all the comments are concatenated. Note that the first comment does not cause the dataset to be malformed, even though it precedes the root element (<car>).

XmlAttributes Property

We've already seen the XmlAttributes property at work in some the examples in this chapter. It's an important property, so we'll look a bit closer.

XmlAttributes is a structure whose members are the attributes of the specified element. Since attributes of an element are name-value pairs, they make perfect candidates for members in a structure.

Like any other ColdFusion structure, we can refer to the values in the XmlAttributes property by their corresponding keys. Sticking with the Simpsons example, let's see how that works.

Using the following code, we can get a list of each person in the family and their corresponding ages:

```
<cfset childCount = ArrayLen(myFamily.people.person)>
<cfloop from="1" to="#childCount#" index="i">
  <cfset thisPerson = myFamily.people.person[i]>
  <cfoutput>
    #thisPerson.XmlAttributes.firstName# - #thisPerson.XmlAttributes.age#<br>
  </cfoutput>
</cfloop>
```

This code results in the following output:

```
Homer - 41
Marge - 39
Bart - 10
Lisa - 8
Maggie - 1
Grandpa - 72
```

CFMX vs. BlueDragon:
As previously noted, BlueDragon also allows the more streamlined notation **thisPerson.firstName** instead of **thisPerson.XmlAttributes.firstName**.

So we have the ability to manipulate XML objects through CFML code and the attributes of the object and its elements. This allows us to take advantage of XML in a wide variety of ways both within and between applications and systems. One of the most popular uses for XML is to transport data to other systems.

Output to Other Systems

I often refer to XML as "the reason ASCII was invented; it just took us 30 years to figure it out". By this I'm referring to the ability of XML to provide an extremely robust, text-based platform for information interchange, fulfilling the "Information Interchange" portion of the ASCII acronym.

We can send data to other systems by formatting it into XML using an agreed-upon vocabulary. The receiving system, being aware of the vocabulary, can readily accept and process the data without a great deal of verification and validation overhead. In order to send such data, we just need to ship out XML data. But that begs what seems to be a simple question: "What is XML data?"

XML Objects Aren't XML Strings

As CFML developers, we need to keep in mind that an XML object in CFML is not the same thing as the XML data expected by other systems. When we talk about transmitting XML data, we are talking about transmitting data encoded in text according to an XML vocabulary.

If we send a CFML XML object directly to another system, errors will occur. This is because XML objects are just programming niceties that exist to help us in the world of CFML code. Other systems don't have any idea what a CFML XML object is, or how to handle it.

To prevent problems in exchanging data with other systems via XML, let's take a look at our Simpsons data as an XML string and as an XML object. Then we'll know we can work safely with external systems.

XML String vs. XML Object

As we've already seen, XML is just text. When we receive XML data from another system, we're receiving text. When we send XML data to another system, we need to send text. It's only in our internal processing that we use CFML XML objects.

We've seen how to convert an XML string into a CFML XML object using the `<cfxml>` tag. We just wrap the XML string with the tag, and assign a value to the `variable` attribute of the tag. A CFML XML object is created and stored under the name specified in the value of the `variable` attribute. What's the difference? Let's take a look.

The following code is a slight variation on the Simpsons example. The variation is that we are first storing the XML data to a string variable before we convert it into an XML object (and we're only using Homer and Marge in this example). This will allow us to compare the two in more detail.

```
<cfscript>
  xmlString = '';
  xmlString = '#xmlString#<people>';
  xmlString = '#xmlString#  <person lastName="Simpson" firstName="Homer" age="41" role="father" />';
  xmlString = '#xmlString#  <person lastName="Simpson" firstName="Marge" age="39" role="mother" />';
  xmlString = '#xmlString#</people>';
</cfscript>

<cfxml variable="xmlObject">
<cfoutput>
#xmlString#
</cfoutput>
</cfxml>

Here's my XML string:<br>
<cfoutput>
#HTMLCodeFormat(xmlString)#
</cfoutput>
<p>
And here's my XML object:<br>
<cfoutput>#HTMLCodeFormat(xmlObject)#</cfoutput>
```

The output from running this code in CFMX looks like this:

```
Here's my XML string:

<people>  <person lastName="Simpson" firstName="Homer" age="41" role="father" />
<person lastName="Simpson" firstName="Marge" age="39" role="mother" /></people>

And here's my XML object:

<?xml version="1.0" encoding="UTF-8"?>

<people>  <person age="41" firstName="Homer" lastName="Simpson" role="father"/>
<person age="39" firstName="Marge" lastName="Simpson" role="mother"/></people>
```

Hang on here. They look very similar, don't they? So why all the scare stories about not sending XML objects to other systems? Let's make sure we know what's happening here.

The XML string output in the first section of output is obviously just the content of the **`xmlString`** variable. But what about the second one? The first thing we notice is that there is an XML declaration added at the beginning of the data. Also, the order of attributes in the data has changed: the attributes are now in alphabetical order within each element. Clearly the server has done something to the data.

When we use `<cfoutput>` on a CFML XML object, the server performs a method that adds the XML declaration and outputs the object's data as text. This makes it very easy to send XML data from a CFML XML object to an outside system: we just use <cfoutput> to generate an XML string.

CFMX vs. BlueDragon:
BlueDragon does not re-order the attributes when generating XML text via <cfoutput>. With the exception of the XML declaration, the BlueDragon output is indistinguishable from the original string (whitespace notwithstanding).

Just to make sure we know what's happening here, let's take a quick reminder of what the XML string and the XML object look like if we examine them with <cfdump>. Here's the code:

```
Here's my XML string:<br>
<cfdump var="#xmlString#">
<p>
And here's my XML object:<br>
<cfdump var="#xmlObject#">
```

And the output is shown in Illustration 6:

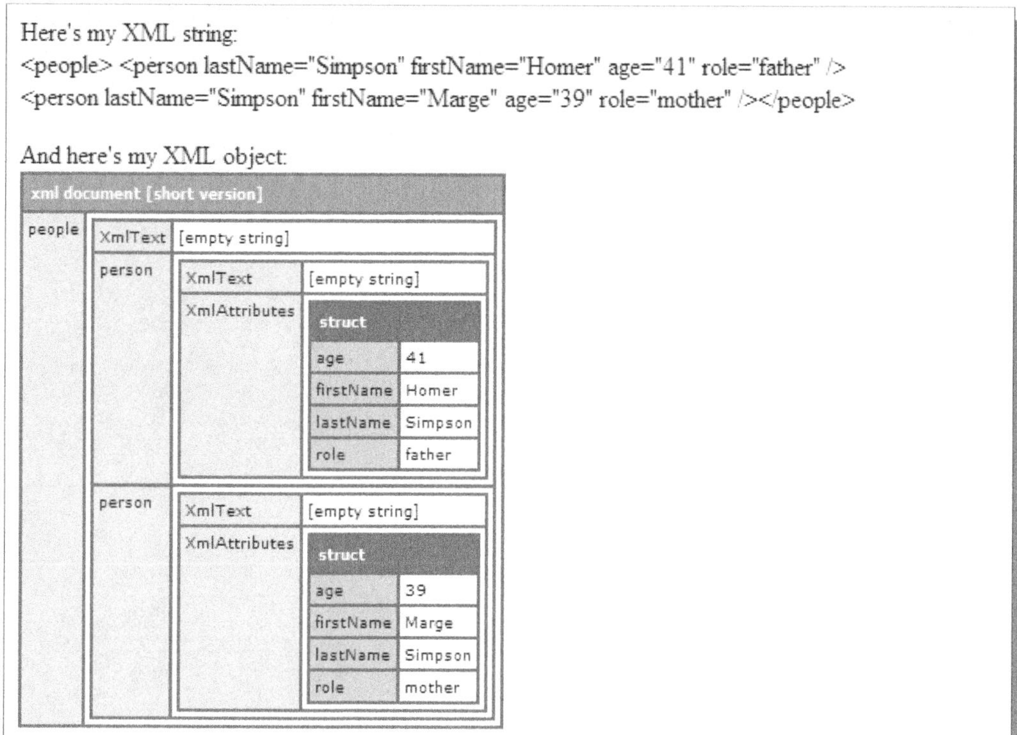

Illustration 6: XML String vs. XML Object <cfdump>

This makes the difference between the XML string and the XML object much more clear. Since non-CFML-based systems have no idea what a CF XML object is, we need to make sure that when we send XML datasets to other systems, we send an XML string and not an XML object.

Summary

With the advent of ColdFusionMX and BlueDragon 6, CFML developers have a strong set of tools for manipulating XML data. XML is a tag-based means for describing and transmitting data within and among applications and systems. XML datasets are plain text. CFML has a special datatype called an XML object that facilitates manipulation of XML data. XML objects and XML strings are not the same thing. When we send data to other systems, XML strings should be sent, not XML objects.

With the basics of XML and XML objects defined, we can move on to explore the use of them in CFML. We'll start with methods for creating XML objects in the next chapter.

Chapter 3 - Creating XML Objects

Introduction

So far we've seen some basic XML manipulation in the context of learning about what XML data is and how CFML defines XML objects. In this chapter we'll explore a variety of methods for creating XML objects, from very simple to more intricate. We'll look at the `<CFXML>` tag, the `XmlParse()` function, the `XmlNew()` function, and finally converting from object to string and back.

<CFXML> Tag

As we saw in the last chapter, the `<CFXML>` tag is an easy way to convert XML data into a CFML XML object. In its most basic use, all we need to do is specify a variable name using the `variable` attribute. An XML object is created with the specified name. The following code results in the XML object shown in Illustration 7:

```
<cfxml variable=”xmlCar”>
  <car make=”Mazda” model=”RX8”>
    <engine type=”rotary” />
    <door side=”left” position=”front” type=”normal” />
    <door side=”left” position=”rear” type=”suicide” />
    <door side=”right” position=”front” type=”normal” />
    <door side=”back” type=”hatch” />
  </car>
</cfxml>

<cfdump var="#xmlCar#">
```

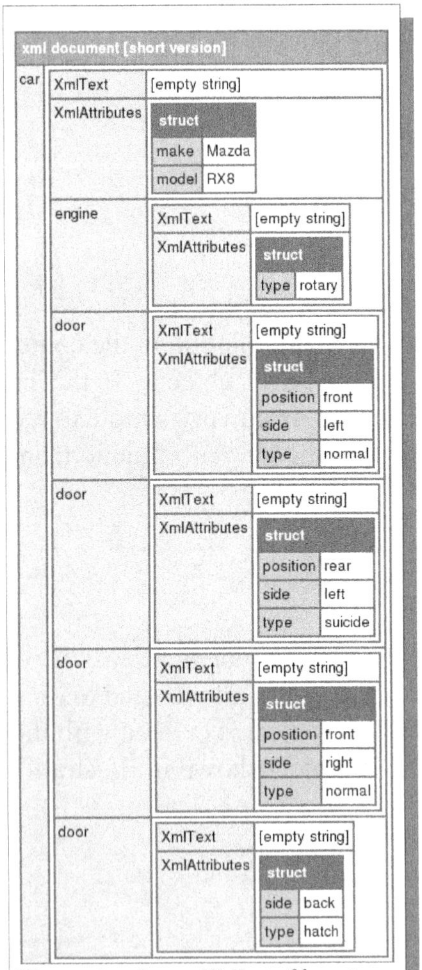

Illustration 7: carXML <cfdump>

The <CFXML> tag can also take the casesensitive attribute. The value of this attribute is a boolean, and it controls whether the elements and attributes in the XML object are differentiated based on case (upper or lower) of the characters in their names. The default value is **no**. To see how this works, let's change the car model a bit so that it has three **door** elements and one **Door** element. The result is shown in Illustration 7:

```
<cfxml variable="xmlCar">
  <car make="Mazda" model="RX8">
    <engine type="rotary" />
    <door side="left" position="front" type="normal" />
    <door side="left" position="rear" type="suicide" />
    <door side="right" position="front" type="normal" />
    <Door side="back" type="hatch" />
  </car>
</cfxml>

<cfdump var="#xmlCar#">
```

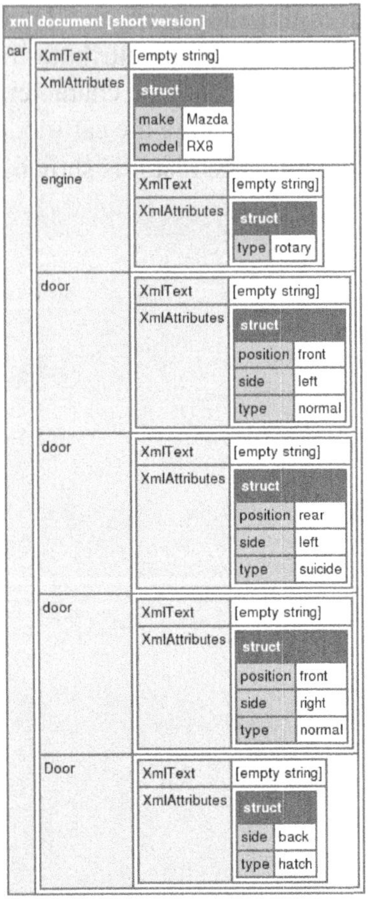

Illustration 8: carXML with Door

This doesn't look much different from the original XML object in Illustration 7. In fact, because the value of the casesensitive attribute is the default—no—there is no functional difference between the two objects. To make this a bit more clear, let's take a look at the result of `<cfdump var="#xmlCar.car.door#">`. It's shown in Illustration 9.

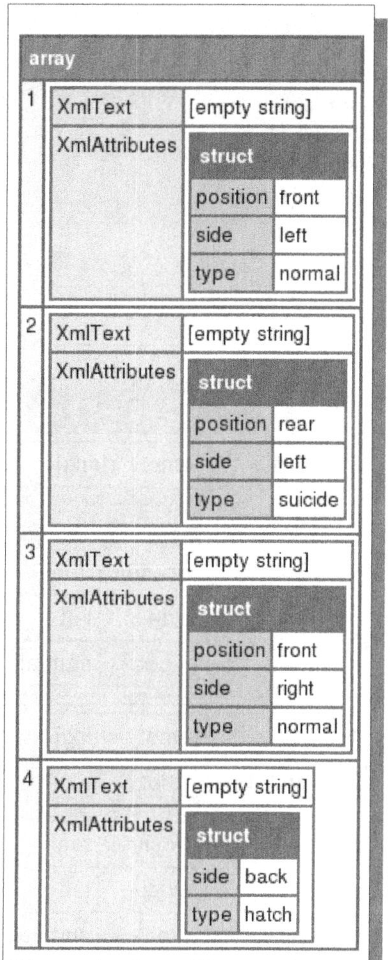

Illustration 9: xmlCar.car.door

Notice that the last element, the one that contains the back hatch, is included in the xmlCar.car.door array. The case of the **Door** element has been ignored. Let's see what happens if we add casesensitive="true" to the <cfxml> tag. The result is shown in Illustration 10.

```
<cfxml variable="xmlCar" casesensitive="true">
  <car make="Mazda" model="RX8">
    <engine type="rotary" />
    <door side="left" position="front" type="normal" />
    <door side="left" position="rear" type="suicide" />
    <door side="right" position="front" type="normal" />
    <Door side="back" type="hatch" />
  </car>
</cfxml>

<cfdump var="#xmlCar.car.door#">
```

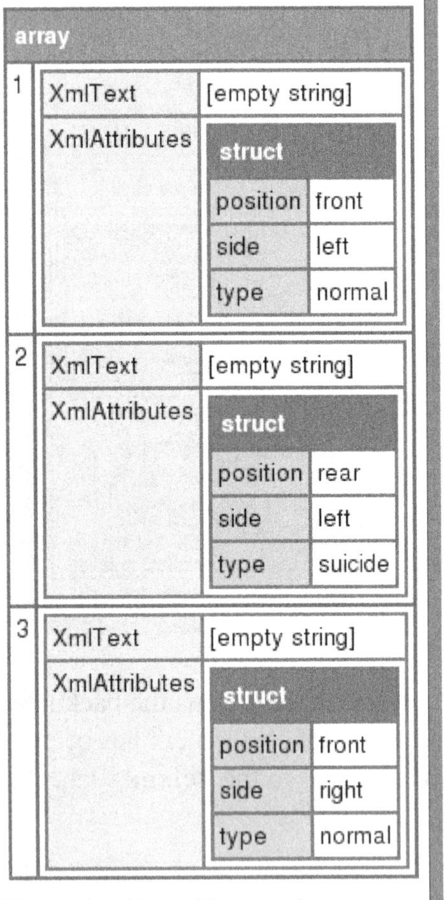

Illustration 10: xmlCar.car.door

Now the **`Door`** element is no longer included in the **`door`** array, because the object is operating in case-sensitive mode.

XML is by definition a case-sensitive language. Therefore, we can avoid problems in transmitting data to other systems if we make our XML objects case-sensitive as a best practice.

So <CFXML> is a very quick and easy way to convert an XML string to an XML object. But there are places where we can't use it. For example, we can't use a tag inside a <CFSCRIPT> block. But there is another method for creating XML objects that can be used in that context. That method is the XmlParse() function.

XmlParse() Function

The XmlParse() function takes two arguments: an XML data string, and an optional boolean for case sensitivity. It returns an XML object.

To illustrate in terms of our existing xmlCar example, let's assume the XML string is contained in a variable named **xmlString**. To create the xmlCar object using the XmlParse() function, we use this syntax:

```
<cfscript>
  xmlCar = XmlParse(xmlString);
</cfscript>
```

Similarly, if we want to create the xmlCar object as a case-sensitive XML object, we just add the argument for case-sensitivity:

```
<cfscript>
  xmlCar = XmlParse(xmlString, true);
</cfscript>
```

XML Processing Directive

A big difference between the <CFXML> tag and the XmlParse() function is that the XmlParse() function will accept an XML processing directive at the beginning of the XML data string. The <CFXML> tag will throw an error if a processing directive is present. Let's change the xmlCar example to add a processing directive:

```
<cfxml variable="xmlCar" casesensitive="true">

 <?xml version="1.0" encoding="UTF-8"?>
 <car make="Mazda" model="RX8">
   <engine type="rotary" />
   <door side="left" position="front" type="normal" />
   <door side="left" position="rear" type="suicide" />
   <door side="right" position="front" type="normal" />
   <Door side="back" type="hatch" />
 </car>
</cfxml>
```

This will throw an error. However, if the same XML string is processed with XmlParse(), it will work without errors. This makes the function ideal for creating XML objects from data contained in files received from other systems.

Parsing XML Data From Files

Since XML data received from an outside source typically has a processing directive at the beginning of the data, the XmlParse() function is an easy way to deal with it. Such data is often stored in a local file before being processed. We can fetch it with <CFFILE> and convert it into an XML object with XmlParse().

Let's say we have an XML data set stored in the file **d:\incomingdata\newCars2006.xml**. We can convert that data into an XML object with the following code:

```
<cffile action="read" file="d:\incomingdata\newCars2006.xml" variable="newCars">
<cfset xmlNewCars=XmlParse(newCars, true)>
```

Using the <CFXML> tag or the XmlParse() function, we can readily turn XML string data into an XML object. That's a good start. Now we need to work on building XML objects from scratch. Fortunately, CFML gives us some functions to do this as well. The first one we need is XmlNew().

XmlNew() Function

For users of CFML, functions ending in New() are nothing new. We have the ArrayNew() function for creating arrays, and the StructNew() function for creating structures. So it should come as no surprise that the XmlNew() function is used to create new XML objects.

As is the case with the other complex datatype creation functions, a variable created with the XmlNew() function has no content. If we run the following code, we'll get an empty XML object, as shown in Illustration 11.

```
<cfset myXMLObj = XmlNew(true)>
<cfdump var="#myXMLObj#">
```

Illustration 11: XmlNew() Result

Clearly, there isn't much use for this XML object in its current state—except, of course, to populate it with data. That's exactly what we need to do next. Fortunately, we can add elements to the object just as easily as we created it.

XmlElemNew() Function

With a blank XML object to work with, we're ready to start adding elements. This is where the XmlElemNew() function comes into play. Using it, we can add an element to the blank object. We can also add elements to other elements, as we'll see in the next few examples.

The XmlElemNew() function takes two arguments: an existing XML object, and a string specifying the name of the element to add. We specify the element to which the new element is being appended by assigning the result of the XmlElemNew() function to that element. In the case of creating the root element, we assign it to the xmlRoot of the XML object.

For starters, we'll add the root node for our car example. As always, the result is shown following the code, in Illustration 12.

```
<cfset xmlCar = XmlNew(true)>
<cfset xmlCar.xmlRoot = XmlElemNew(xmlCar, "car")>
<cfdump var="#xmlCar#">
```

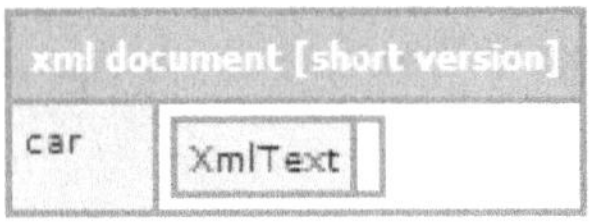

Illustration 12: XmlElemNew() Result

Now we can use the XmlElemNew() function to add the rest of the elements in the car dataset, as shown below. The end result in Illustration 8 is an XML object that looks just like the one we created with the <CFXML> tag (shown in Illustration 7).

```
<cfset xmlCar = XmlNew()>
<cfset xmlCar.xmlRoot = XmlElemNew(xmlCar, "car")>
<cfset xmlCar.car.XmlAttributes["make"] = "Mazda">
<cfset xmlCar.car.XmlAttributes["model"] = "RX8">
<cfset xmlCar.car.XmlChildren[1] = XmlElemNew(xmlCar, "engine")>
<cfset xmlCar.car.engine.XmlAttributes["type"] = "rotary">
<cfloop from="2" to="5" index="i">
 <cfset xmlCar.car.XmlChildren[i] = XmlElemNew(xmlCar, "door")>
 <cfif i LT 4>
  <cfset xmlCar.car.door[i-1].XmlAttributes["side"] = "left">
 <cfelseif i LT 5>
  <cfset xmlCar.car.door[i-1].XmlAttributes["side"] = "right">
 <cfelse>
  <cfset xmlCar.car.door[i-1].XmlAttributes["side"] = "back">
 </cfif>
</cfloop>
<cfset xmlCar.car.door[1].XmlAttributes["position"] = "front">
<cfset xmlCar.car.door[1].XmlAttributes["type"] = "normal">
<cfset xmlCar.car.door[2].XmlAttributes["position"] = "rear">
<cfset xmlCar.car.door[2].XmlAttributes["type"] = "suicide">
<cfset xmlCar.car.door[3].XmlAttributes["position"] = "front">
<cfset xmlCar.car.door[3].XmlAttributes["type"] = "normal">
<cfset xmlCar.car.door[4].XmlAttributes["type"] = "hatch">

<cfdump var="#xmlCar#">
```

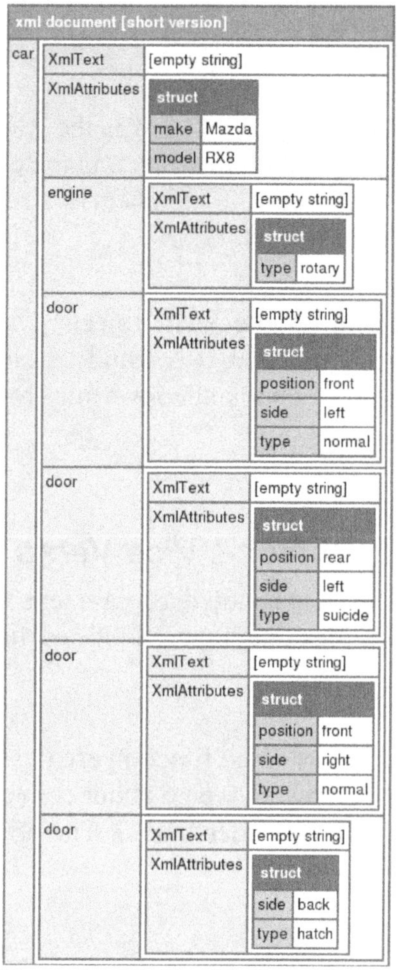

Illustration 13: Hand-built xmlCar

Before we leave this topic, let's take a look at the syntax in the code before Illustration 8. In particular, we're interested in the lines that set values for attributes. They are easily identified by the presence of the XmlAttributes keyword. The syntax in these statements shows how the attributes collection for a given element is treated as a structure named **`XmlAttributes`**. To add a new attribute, we just set a value for it using bracketed notation as we could with a regular structure. We could also use dot notation.

NOTE: Early versions of CFMX were finicky about dot notation with XmlAttributes. Bracket notation is safer if we're using version prior to CFMX 7.

Another similar treatment from a code point of view is the way we reference elements of the same type. The type name is treated as an array, and the elements are reference by index number, just as we would reference the members of a regular array. Thus, in the care example, `xmlCar.door[1]` refers to the front left door.

We now have a few different ways to create XML objects: the `<CFXML>` tag, the `XmlParse()` function for parsing XML strings, and the `XMLNew()` and `XmlElemNew()` functions for building XML objects from scratch. Let's take a look at converting from an XML string to an XML object and back.

Converting XML to XML Object & Vice Versa

In the world outside of CFML, XML is handled as plain text. Inside CFML, we can take advantage of the XML object complex data type. So it's useful to recognize a few ways to convert from one to the other.

Of course, the `<CFXML>` tag and the `XmlParse()` function are the ways we can convert XML text into a CFML XML object. So how do we go about converting a CFML XML object into XML text that the rest of the world understands? The primary means are the `<CFOUTPUT>` tag and the `ToString()` method.

Plain Old <CFOUTPUT>

One of the nice things about the way ColdFusion and BlueDragon handle XML objects is that they allow us to simply use the <CFOUTPUT> tag to convert an XML object into and XML string. Let's take a look at how each platform does this.

We'll use our xmlCar example from earlier in the chapter. The code to generate an XML string from the object is simply this:

```
<cfoutput>#xmlCar#</cfoutput>
```

The result of this code as presented by ColdFusion looks like this:

```
<?xml version="1.0" encoding="UTF-8"?>
<car make="Mazda" model="RX8">
    <engine type="rotary"/>
    <door position="front" side="left" type="normal"/>
    <door position="rear" side="left" type="suicide"/>
    <door position="front" side="right" type="normal"/>
    <door side="back" type="hatch"/>
  </car>
```

Notice that when we use <CFOUTPUT>, the XML processing directive gets added at the top of the XML string. Now let's look at the output from BlueDragon:

```
<?xml version="1.0" encoding="UTF-8"?>
<car make="Mazda" model="RX8">
    <engine type="rotary"/>
    <door side="left" position="front" type="normal"/>
    <door side="left" position="rear" type="suicide"/>
    <door side="right" position="front" type="normal"/>
    <door side="back" type="hatch"/>
  </car>
```

There's a very subtle difference in the two XML strings. ColdFusion has arranged the attributes for each element in alphabetical order, whereas BlueDragon represents the attributes in the same order in which they were created.

This difference is not significant in the world of XML, where one of the rules is that the order of attributes does not affect the data.

One final note on using <CFOUTPUT> to generate XML strings: the output reproduced in the above examples was revealed by using the browser's View Source command. If we want to use <CFOUTPUT> to generate an XML string for sending to an outside system, we need to capture the result in a variable. This is easily done with the <CFSAVECONTENT> tag:

```
<cfsavecontent variable="carXMLString">
 <cfoutput>#xmlCar#</cfoutput>
</cfsavecontent>
```

As was the case with <CFXML>, we can't use <CFOUTPUT> and <CFSAVECONTENT> within a <CFSCRIPT> block. So there's another way we can convert and XML object into an XML string: the ToString() function.

ToString() Function

In CFML, the ToString() function converts a non-string piece of data into a string representation of the data. It takes two arguments: the value to be converted into a string, and and optional string to specify the encoding to be used. The default encoding is the encoding of the page from which the function is called. We can look at what it does with this bit of code:

```
<cfoutput>#ToString(xmlCar)#</cfoutput>
```

The result of doing this is exactly the same as doing <cfoutput>#xmlCar#</cfoutput>, including the XML processing directive.

So what's the point of having a ToString() function if <CFOUTPUT> already does the same thing? This is where we go back to <CFSCRIPT> and other places where expressions are processed.

To start, we know that we can't use tags within a <CFSCRIPT> block. Knowing that <CFOUTPUT> around an XML object returns an XML string, we might be tempted to do the following in a script block:

```
<cfscript>
  xmlCarString = xmlCar;
</cfscript>
```

But that code just sets the variable **xmlCarString** to point to the **xmlCar** variable, so **xmlCarString** behaves as an XML object, not as a string. We can test this by using <CFDUMP var="#xmlCarString#"> after the script. The result is shown in Illustration 13.

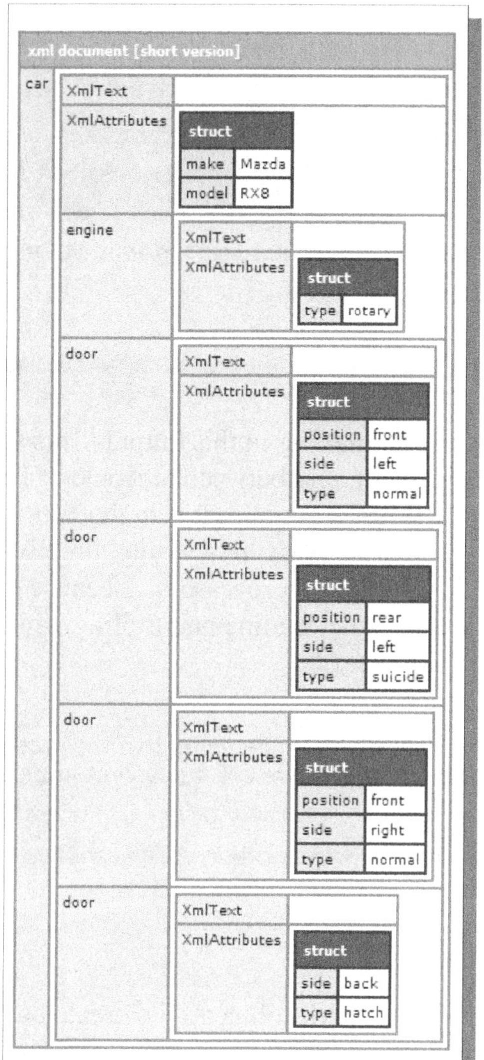

Illustration 14: xmlCarString <cfdump>

Clearly, the result of the code is an XML object, not an XML string as we wanted. So a small change to take advantage of the tostring() function will provide the result we want. Here's the code:

```
<cfscript>
  xmlCarString = ToString(xmlCar);
</cfscript>
```

And the result is this:

<?xml version="1.0" encoding="UTF-8"?> <car make="Mazda" model="RX8"> <engine type="rotary"/> <door position="front" side="left" type="normal"/> <door position="rear" side="left" type="suicide"/> <door position="front" side="right" type="normal"/> <door side="back" type="hatch"/> </car>

Illustration 15: ToString(xmlCar) <cfdump>

Notice that there is no nice code formatting in this output. It is stripped of all whitespace except a space between each element, and between attributes. This makes it ideal for transmittal to outside systems. 'What is not apparent in the <CFOUTPUT> examples is that there are two blank lines preceding the XML processing directive at the top of the dataset. This can cause problems with some XML processors. Because of this, it's good to be in the habit of using the Trim() function to strip leading and trailing whitespace from XML strings before sending them to other processes.

CFMX vs. BlueDragon: BlueDragon also implements tostring() as a method of the XML document object. So the following statements are equivalent in BlueDragon:

```
<cfset myVar = tostring(xmlCar)>
<cfset myVar = xmlCar.tostring()>
```

Summary

CFML offers several ways to create XML objects. To create an XML object from an existing XML string, we can use the <CFXML> tag or the XmlParse() function. To create an XML object from scratch, we can use the XmlNew() function. To add elements to an XML object, we can use the XmlElemNew() function.

Generating an XML string from an XML object is also very straightforward. We can use the <CFOUTPUT> tag on an XML object. We can also use the ToString() function to return a string representation of an XML object.

Once we have an XML object created, we need to be able to do something with the data inside it. In the next chapter, we'll look at how to use XML Stylesheet Language

Transformation (XSLT) to generate output using XML. We'll also briefly revisit the `ToString()` function from an output perspective.

Chapter 4 - Output From XML Objects

Introduction

In the previous chapter, we explored ways to create XML objects in CFML, both from existing XML data and from scratch. In this chapter, we're going to look at using the data in XML objects. There are two primary ways to do this: first, treating the XML object as a complex data type and extracting data using CFML manipulation; and second, using XML Stylesheet Language Transformation (XSLT) to manipulate XML string data.

While the latter approach has an enormous amount of power, and has the advantages of being standards-based, the former approach will be more immediately familiar to CFML developers. So we'll visit XSLT a bit later on. For now, we'll start by addressing various data points within an XML object.

In order to illustrate the techniques in this chapter, we'll use a new XML dataset. Here it is:

```
<pokerTable number="4005678">Welcome to our feature table.
 <hand>
   <card suit="spades" value="K" />
   <card suit="spades" value="10" />
 </hand>
 <hand>
   <card suit="hearts" value="A" />
   <card suit="clubs" value="A" />
 </hand>
 <hand>
   <card suit="diamonds" value="Q" />
   <card suit="spades" value="5" />
 </hand>
 <hand>
   <card suit="clubs" value="8" />
   <card suit="clubs" value="9" />
 </hand>
 <hand>
   <card suit="hearts" value="2" />
   <card suit="diamonds" value="10" />
 </hand>
</pokerTable>
```

Throughout this chapter, we'll refer to this XML data as the XML object `pokerTableXML`.

Looping and XML Objects

Since an XML object in CFML is essentially a structure whose keys are either themselves structures, arrays of structures, or simple datatypes, we can use familiar CFML syntax to look into an XML object's data. The key to the whole game is in knowing how to address elements, attributes, and text within the XML data. Once we have those basic tools, we can also loop over an element, a set of elements, or an element's attributes. The following sections cover these techniques.

Referencing an Element

XML objects in CFML are essentially structures. Thanks to this, we can use the familiar syntaxes for referencing data in structures to reference elements in XML objects. So, the code `<cfdump var="#pokerTableXML.pokerTable#">` would return the **`pokerTable`** element, which looks like Illustration 16 (the vertical table has been broken into three sections to save page space).

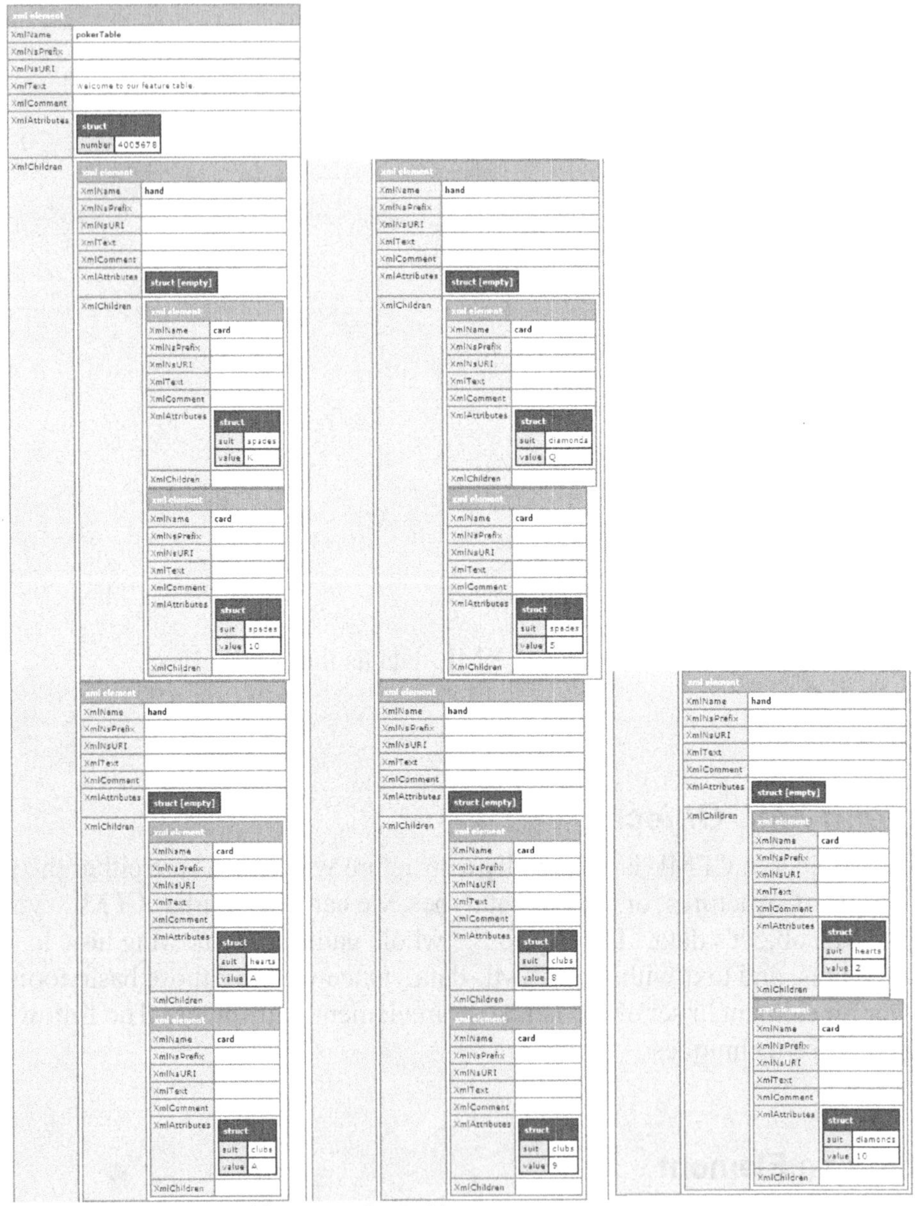

Illustration 16: pokerTableXML.pokerTable

Don't worry about the details too much; the point is just that the pokerTable element within the pokerTableXML structure is itself a structure. We'll be building from there.

Thanks to this structures-within-structures nature of XML objects in CFML, referencing any element within the XML object is quite simple using basic dotted notation. All we do is delimit element names with dots to return the desired element.

But elements aren't the only aspect to XML data. We also have attributes to manage.

Referencing an Attribute

Where elements appear as tags within an XML dataset, attributes appear as the familiar name-value pairs within opening tags. When we reference attributes in a CFML XML object, we have to take a slightly different approach than the one we use for elements.

An element's attributes are contained within a structure named XmlAttributes. Let's say we want to find out the value of the number attribute of the pokerTable element in our sample XML object. We can reference that attribute with the variable name `pokerTableXML.pokerTable.XmlAttributes["number"]`. The result is the value **`4005678`**.

> **CFMX vs. BlueDragon**
> BlueDragon allows the use of dot notation to refer to attributes as well as elements, obviating the need for explicit references to the XmlAttributes structure. Where the example above will work in BlueDragon, we can also use the simpler syntax `pokerTableXML.pokerTable.number`.

Referencing an Element's Text

Many XML vocabularies opt to use elements to name data, and text within elements to contain the actual data. In cases like this, the general construct looks like this: <elementName>value</elementName>. Using this method, the value is referred to as the element's text. According to the XML standard, an element's text is defined as anything inside the element that is not another element or a comment.

In our sample data, the string **`Welcome to our feature table.`** is the text for the pokerTable element.

CFML uses the XmlText variable to refer to the text of an XML element. So getting the text from the pokerTable element is done by using the variable name `pokerTableXML.pokerTable.XmlText`. The returned value is all the text contained inside the element, not including elements or comments. So if we had put more text inside the closing tag (</pokerTable>), it would be returned as part of the XmlText as well.

There is also a shortcut for referencing the XmlText of an element when using <CFOUTPUT>. When referencing an element, <CFOUTPUT> defaults to the XmlText key if no other is specified. Consequently, the following two statements are equivalent:

```
<cfoutput>#pokerTableXML.pokerTable.XmlText#</cfoutput>
<cfoutput>#pokerTableXML.pokerTable#</cfoutput>
```

Bear in mind, though, that this equivalence does not hold true outside the use of <CFOUTPUT>. After all, pokerTable is a structure, whereas XmlText is a string. The difference can be seen if we repeat the two statements above using <CFDUMP> instead.

```
<cfdump var="#pokerTableXML.pokerTable.XmlText#">
<cfdump var="#pokerTableXML.pokerTable#">
```

The first statement returns the expected text. As we saw in Illustration 16, the latter statement returns the **pokerTable** element, which is a fairly lengthy structure.

With the ability to reference elements and attributes, we can move on to more complex reference situations. In most cases when dealing with XML, we need to loop over sets of data to get the results we want. The next sections will deal with looping over an element and sets of elements.

Looping Over An Element

As we've noted already, an element within a CFML XML object is a structure. It contains some built-in keys like XmlName, and other keys that may or may not exist depending on the contents of the element. For example, if the element has attributes, they will be contained within a key named XmlAttributes, which is itself a structure. Similarly, elements within the element will be represented as structures.

Therefore, looping over the contents of an element is as easy as looping over a structure. However, XML objects are treated a bit differently from generic structures when it comes to looping behavior. The following code loops over the pokerTableXML.pokerTable element, reporting the name of each key it finds.

```
<cfloop collection="#pokerTableXML.pokerTable#" item="thisNode">
  <cfoutput>
  This node is named #thisNode#.<br>
  </cfoutput>
</cfloop>
```

The result of this code is five lines that each read **This node is named hand.** Even though other keys are present, such as **XmlAttributes**, they are ignored when looping over the XML object. The looping mechanism only recognizes elements.

This behavior can be quite beneficial, as it allows us to deal only with the data specified in the XML dataset when using looping constructs. The other keys are actually meta-data added in by the application server to make our lives a bit easier. So it makes sense that loops should ignore the meta-data, leaving it available only if we specifically request it. For example, we can ask for the **XmlAttributes** key in the **pokerTable** element:

```
<cfdump var="#pokerTableXML.pokerTable.XmlAttributes#">
```

This will return the **XmlAttributes** key's value, which is itself a structure, as shown in Illustration 17.

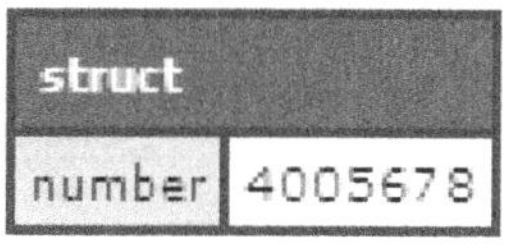

Illustration 17: pokerTable.XmlAttributes

Often in the world of XML, a dataset will include several elements of the same name. In our poker example, we have five elements all named **hand**, and each **hand** element contains two elements named **card**. If we refer to the element named **pokerTableXML.pokerTable.hand**, we'll always get the first element named hand inside the **pokerTable** element.

To be able to deal with such recurring elements, we need a way to refer to the individual members of the the set. We'll explore this a bit in the next section.

Looping Over a Set of Elements

When two or more elements of the same name are found within an XML object as siblings (that is, they are contained by the same parent element), they can be treated as an array of structures, numbered in the order in which they appear in the dataset.

Thus, the five occurrences of the **hand** element in our example can be referenced as **pokerTableXML.pokerTable.hand[1]**
..
pokerTableXML.pokerTable.hand[5].

And we can loop over the **hand** element just as though it were any other array in CFML. The output for the following code can be found in Illustration 18 (output spliced in parallel sections to save page space).

```
<cfloop from="1" to="#ArrayLen(pokerTableXML.pokerTable.hand)#" index="i">
  <cfdump var="#pokerTableXML.pokerTable.hand[i]#" label="Hand #i#">
</cfloop>
```

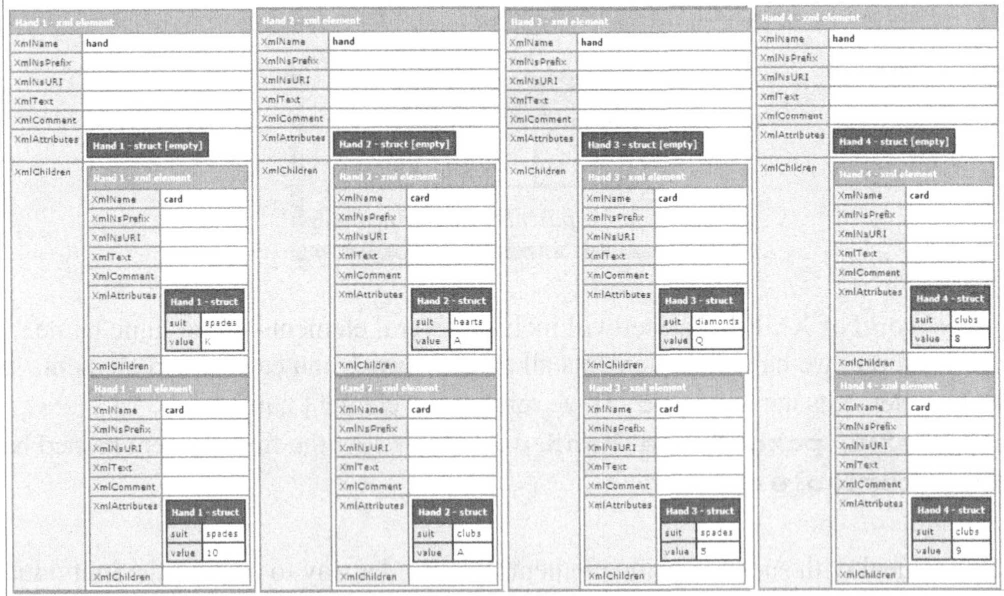

Illustration 18: Looped dump of pokerTable.hands

Curiously, though, while a set of elements operates like an array, and can be looped over like an array, it is not really an array, according to CFML. Thus, the expression IsArray(pokerTableXML.pokerTable.hand) will return **NO**, even though we can loop over it like an array, and use array functions like ArrayLen() on it.

In fact, the ArrayLen() function will work on any element in an XML object, regardless of whether it is in a multi-element set. In other words, ArrayLen(pokerTableXML.pokerTable) would return `1`. So in cases where we might have one or many occurrences of a particular element, it's safe to create a loop based on ArrayLen() to deal with them; there will be no error generated if there is only one occurrence.

As a final demonstration of looping over elements, the following code loops over the hands in our pokerTable, and the cards in each hand, and displays their values for our review. The output is in Illustration 19.

```
<table border="1">
<tr>
<cfloop from="1" to="#ArrayLen(pokerTableXML.pokerTable.hand)#" index="h">
  <cfoutput><td width="100">Hand #h#:<br></cfoutput>
  <cfloop from="1" to="#ArrayLen(pokerTableXML.pokerTable.hand[h].card)#" index="c">
    <cfoutput>
      #pokerTableXML.pokerTable.hand[h].card[c].XmlAttributes["value"]#
      #pokerTableXML.pokerTable.hand[h].card[c].XmlAttributes["suit"]#<br>
    </cfoutput>
  </cfloop>
  </td><br>
</cfloop>
</tr>
</table>
```

Hand 1: K spades 10 spades	Hand 2: A hearts A clubs	Hand 3: Q diamonds 5 spades	Hand 4: 8 clubs 9 clubs	Hand 5: 2 hearts 10 diamonds

Illustration 19: Card values from nested loop

Just as we can loop over sets of elements, we can also loop over the set of attributes within an element. The next section explores this common task.

Looping Over an Element's Attributes

We've seen the XmlAttributes key in an element's structure before. It is itself a structure, and it carries the name/value pairs encoded in the element's attributes. So looping over an element's attributes becomes as easy an exercise as looping over its elements.

The following code is a slight modification to the previous example. This time we use the XmlAttributes collection to get the desired output. Note how this cuts down on the hard-coded nature of the program. The output is shown in Illustration 20.

```
<table border="1">
<tr>
<cfloop from="1" to="#ArrayLen(pokerTableXML.pokerTable.hand)#" index="h">
  <td width="100">
  <cfloop from="1" to="#ArrayLen(pokerTableXML.pokerTable.hand[h].card)#" index="c">
    <cfset thisCard = pokerTableXML.pokerTable.hand[h].card[c]>
    <cfloop collection="#thisCard.XmlAttributes#" item="thisAttribute">
      <cfoutput>
        #thisAttribute# is #thisCard.XmlAttributes[thisAttribute]#<br>
      </cfoutput>
    </cfloop>
  </cfloop>
  </td>
</cfloop>
</tr>
</table>
```

suit is spades value is K suit is spades value is 10	suit is hearts value is A suit is clubs value is A	suit is diamonds value is Q suit is spades value is 5	suit is clubs value is 8 suit is clubs value is 9	suit is hearts value is 2 suit is diamonds value is 10

Illustration 20: Output from looping over XmlAttributes

Clearly we have a great deal of control over how we can manipulate the data constained within a CFML XML object. We can do just about anything we please using CFML code and the techniques in this chapter to reference the data. But we've only begun to scratch the surface with respect to the power of using XML data, particularly when it comes to generating output from XML.

One of the most powerful capabilities of XML is its ability to be transformed into practically any output format we want. From an XML dataset, we can generate comma-delimited data, HTML, documentation pages, forms, or even another XML dataset, using an XML-specific technique called Extensible Stylesheet Language Transformation (XSLT). The stylesheets used in this process are called XSL stylesheets. There is a function in CFML that performs XSL transformations for us; the next section contains an introduction to it.

XmlTransform() Function

The XmlTransform() function in CFML takes three arguments: an XML data string; an XSL stylesheet as a string, a relative path to a stylesheet file, or a URL; and an optional structure containing parameters for the stylesheet to use. It returns the result of the processed XSL transformation.

One of the most important things to note about the XmlTransform() function is that it does NOT operate only on CFML XML objects. The first argument can be an XML object OR an XML data string. Consequently, if we're using XmlTransform(), we don't need to use the <CFXML> tag or the XmlParse() function to convert and existing XML string into and XML object. Likewise, if we build an XML object from scratch, we don't need to convert it into an XML string before using XmlTransform() on it. Very handy indeed.

For all its power, the XmlTransform() function is very simple to use. The much more complex aspect comes in when we start building the XSL stylesheets required for use with it. The next sections will take an introductory look at XSLT and some of the implications of using it as opposed to sticking purely to CFML code.

An XSLT Primer

Just as Cascading Style Sheet (CSS) stylesheets provide instructions to a browser for rendering content, XSL stylesheets provide instructions to an XSLT engine for performing transformations. Generally speaking, they contain statements of the “when you find string A, output string B” variety. They can, however, get quite complex, not only transforming strings but managing calculations on the way through and producing output based on the results. XSLT is a topic which can (and has) occupied books much larger than this one.

So our task here is to get a solid basic understanding of XSLT and look at a few simple stylesheets so we're better able to leverage this powerful tool in our CFML applications. First we'll take a look at why we'd want to use XSL in the first place. Then we'll look at how XSL stylesheets work, with a simple XSL stylesheet based on our poker example, followed by some practical XSLT applications.

Why Use XSLT?

The previous chapters have provided us with very powerful ways to manipulate XML-based data in CFML. It may seem as though we don't really need another way to create output from CFML. Essentially everything we can accomplish with XSLT can be accomplished through CFML code. While this is true on its face, there are a few very good reasons for being able to support XSLT from within ColdFusion.

One of the most persuasive reasons for using XSLT instead of a custom CFML program is the standardized nature of XSL. Because XML and XSL are well-known standards, the XSL stylesheets we create can be used by any transformation engine, not just the one within ColdFusion or BlueDragon. Though we may or may not ever use the same stylesheet in a different environment, the skills used in writing stylesheets for use within CFML application are the same skills we would use for XSLT on any other platform. So our development efforts are far more useful to us over the long run.

XSL transformations are also much simpler from the perspective of readability in our CFML applications. Consider the following code, which converts an XML string into a CFML XML object, then loops over the object to generate a comma-delimited dataset and save the results to a variable:

```
<cfxml variable="myXMLObj">
  <employees>
    <employee lastname="Doe" firstname="John" empID="1" />
    <employee lastname="Public" firstname="Jane" empID="2" />
    <employee lastname="Smith" firstname="Bob" empID="3" />
  </employees>
</cfxml>

<cfset crlf = "#Chr(13)##Chr(10)#">

<cfsavecontent variable="csvData">
  <cfoutput>
    "lastName","firstName","empID"#crlf#
    <cfloop from="1" to="#ArrayLen(myXMLObj.employees.employee)#" index="i">
      "#myXMLObj.employees.employee[i].XmlAttributes.lastName#","#myXMLObj.employees.employee[i].Xml
Attributes.firstName#",#myXMLObj.employees.employee[i].XmlAttributes.empID##crlf#
    </cfloop>
  </cfoutput>
</cfsavecontent>
```

The content of the csvData variable looks like this:

```
"lastName","firstName","empID"
"Doe","John",1
"Public","Jane",2
"Smith","Bob",3
```

Now compare that with the CFML command to perform an XSL transformation on the same XML string (in the variable xmlString:

```
<cffile action="read" file="c:\XSL\empCSV.xsl" variable="xslSheet">
<cfset csvData = xmlTransform(xmlString, xslSheet)>
```

Note that we're not comparing the code that does the transformation itself, as that's in the XSL stylesheet, which is not shown in the example. Rather, the point is that it's much easier to see the intent of the program, from the perspective of the CFML code. The XSL code in the empCSV.xsl file tranforms the XML into the comma-delimited data. We'll look at that style sheet's code in the next section.

Even though using XSLT means learning a new "programming language", the conventions of the language aren't far removed from things we use regularly in other tag-based languages. That means we can focus on how the language works, rather than the mechanics of tags, attributes, and so on.

Though XSLT is a subject that can occupy volumes much larger than this one, we can at least look at the basics of how XSL stylesheets work, and begin to incorporate them into our CFML applications.

How XSL Stylesheets Work

An XSL stylesheet is, like other programs, just a set of instructions. At its simplest, a stylesheet just goes through an XML dataset and looks for elements and/or attributes. When it finds a specific element or attribute, it writes out the specified content, optionally including the value of the element or attribute.

In some ways, the tranformation process is like translating from one written language to another. For example, when translating from English to German, if we encounter the string "car", we "tranform" it to the string "das Auto". (Obviously, the job of translating languages is not nearly this simple, but you get the picture.) We can also do things like maintain running totals or perform complex calculations across an XML dataset. These techniques can be found in any of the many general references on XML that are on the market.

So the basic process behind XSL Transformation is to provide an XML dataset and an XSL stylesheet, and process the dataset through the stylesheet using an XSLT engine. The XSLT engine in CFML is the `XmlTransform()` function. Let's take a look at some basic tranformations, and some practical applications for XSLT in CFML.

Some Practical XSLT Applications

In the previous section, we looked at a process for converting an XML dataset into a comma-delimited dataset. This is an application you might want to use in any of a variety of situations, so we'll explore it a bit in this section.

Converting to CSV

First, let's look at the empCSV.xsl stylesheet we used earlier.

```
<?xml version='1.0'?>
<xsl:stylesheet version="1.0" xmlns:xsl="http://www.w3.org/1999/XSL/Transform">

<xsl:template match="/employees">lastName,firstName,empID<xsl:apply-templates select="employee" />
</xsl:template>
<xsl:template match="employee">
"<xsl:value-of select="@lastname" />","<xsl:value-of select="@firstname" />",<xsl:value-of select="@empID"
/>
</xsl:template>

</xsl:stylesheet>
```

Taking the stylesheet apart a few lines at a time, we can see that its job is really nothing mystical at all. The first line declares the XML version, since XSL is an XML vocabulary. The next line specifies the stylesheet version and the namespace URL. The real work begins after these first two lines.

```
<xsl:template match="/employees">lastName,firstName,empID<xsl:apply-templates select="employee" />
</xsl:template>
```

These two lines define a template block that says, "for every element named `employees` under the root node, write out the text **`lastName,firstName,empID`**, then process any children named `employee` using the template block defined for that node name."

```
<xsl:template match="employee">
"<xsl:value-of select="@lastname" />","<xsl:value-of select="@firstname" />",<xsl:value-of select="@empID"
/>
</xsl:template>
```

These lines define another template block, this time for elements named `employee`. For each such element, the stylesheet will write a double-quote, followed by the value of the `lastname` attribute, followed by a double-quote-comma-double-quote string, the value of the `firstname` attribute, double-quote-comma string, and the value of the `empID` attribute.

```
</xsl:stylesheet>
```

Finally, the last line closes the `xsl:stylesheet` tag. When this stylesheet is applied to the XML data we saw earlier, the result is a comma-separated dataset with field names in the first row.

Output as HTML

One of the most frequent uses for XSLT is to tranform XML data into displayable HTML. Here's a stylesheet to display the employees data in an HTML table:

```
<?xml version='1.0'?>
<xsl:stylesheet version="1.0" xmlns:xsl="http://www.w3.org/1999/XSL/Transform">
<xsl:output method="html" doctype-public="-//W3C//DTD HTML 4.0 Transitional//EN" />

<xsl:template match="/employees">
<table border="1">
  <tr>
    <th>Last Name</th>
    <th>First Name</th>
    <th>Employee ID</th>
  </tr>
  <xsl:apply-templates select="employee" />
</table>
</xsl:template>

<xsl:template match="employee">
  <tr>
    <td><xsl:value-of select="@lastname" /></td>
    <td><xsl:value-of select="@firstname" /></td>
    <td><xsl:value-of select="@empID" /></td>
  </tr>
</xsl:template>

</xsl:stylesheet>
```

A transformation using this stylesheet results in the simple table shown in Illustration 21.

Last Name	First Name	Employee ID
Doe	John	1
Public	Jane	2
Smith	Bob	3

Illustration 21: Transformed HTML Table

Other Practical Applications

The two practical examples shown here just scratch the surface of what's possible with

XSL transformations. Hopefully, the differences between the two examples help illustrate the open potential of using XSLT in your applications. Essentially, XSLT allows us to transform XML data into just about any sort of output we'd like. We can even transform data encoded in one XML vocabulary into a different vocabulary. In Chapter 8, we'll use XSLT on the XML vocabularies used in Fusebox.

With the power of XSLT processing available, let's take a quick look back at the ToString() function, this time with an eye toward XSLT.

Revisiting the ToString() Function

As we saw in previous chapters, the ToString() function is a very simple way to get an XML string representation of the data in a CFML XML object. Knowing this, we might take advantage of the function to process XML objects using XSLT.

For example, if we have an XML object named employeesXML, and we want to transform it using the stylesheet in the file c:\XSL\timesheets.xsl, we could use the following code:

```
<cfset xmlString = ToString(employeesXML)>
<cffile action="read" file="c:\XSL\timesheets.xsl" variable="xslSheet">
<cfset timesheetHTML = XmlTransform(xmlString, xslSheet)>
```

The ToString() function renders the employeesXML object as an XML string, which is then be processed using the XmlTransform() function.

However, this extra step is not necessary, because the XmlTransform() function can take either an XML string or an XML object as its first argument. Thus, this code works just as well:

```
<cffile action="read" file="c:\XSL\timesheets.xsl" variable="xslSheet">
<cfset timesheetHTML = XmlTransform(employeesXML, xslSheet)>
```

NOTE: The XmlTransform() and ToString() functions both supply the XML directive **<?xml version="1.0" encoding="UTF-8"?>** at the beginning of their output, if it is not already there. Consequently, if XmlTransform() is used to create non-XML output (such as the earlier CSV example), the XML directive must be removed from the result.

Summary

CFML gives us a variety of ways to produce output from XML objects. Because of their structure-based nature, we can loop over elements, set of attributes, and sets of elements within an XML object with normal CFML looping logic. We can also use the ToString() function to generate an XML string representation of an XML object. Finally, we can use the XmlTransform() function to leverage the power of XSL stylesheets against an XML object.

This chapter has focused primarily on generating output from an entire XML object. In the next chapter, we'll look at extracting specific pieces of data from an XML object.

Chapter 5 - Getting Data from XML Objects

Introduction

In the previous chapter, we looked at how to output XML objects in whole, and how to loop over sections of XML objects. This chapter takes up more direct data access, looking at addressing specific data points within an XML object, and using the XPath standard to extract data from an XML string. We'll start with techniques to output a single datapoint within an XML object.

Output One Item

We started looking at the idea of addressing single datapoints in an XML object in the last chapter, when we were looping and outputting data. The addressing scheme within an XML object is closely related to the addressing we use for nested structures, with a couple of exceptions. This section will look at this addressing scheme, including the exceptions.

For purposes of discussion in this section, we'll use the following XML dataset:

```
<sealife>
  <fish>Fish have gills.<!-- True for all fish? -->
    <organism popularname="bluefish">Good sport fishing</organism>
    <organism popularname="shark">Fun fishing and some are good to eat</organism>
  </fish>
  <mollusks>
    <organism popularname="mussel">Alive, alive oh</organism>
    <organism popularname="clam">Not to be confused with oysters</organism>
    <organism popularname="scallop">Like the Shell Oil sign</organism>
  </mollusks>
  <mammals>
    <organism popularname="porpoise">They call him Flipper...</organism>
    <organism popularname="sea lion">I like these better than seals</organism>
    <organism popularname="human">
      Found on beaches in summer
      <!-- This should be removed. People aren't sealife! -->

    </organism>
  </mammals>
</sealife>
```

We'll store this dataset in an XML object variable name **sealifeXML**.

Get an Element

Elements are referenced using structure dot notation. The basic reference for an element is just its hierarchical path within the XML data, delimited by dots. So, in our example dataset, we can refer to the fish element with the variable name sealifeXML.sealife.fish.

If there are more than one of a given element, the elements are treated as an array, but it's bit more complex than just using an array. The non-indexed reference sealifeXML.sealife.fish.organism returns the content shown in Illustration 22.

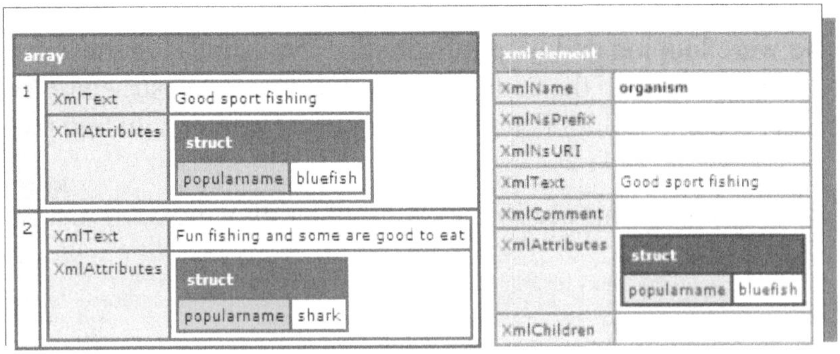

CFMX vs. BlueDragon: CFMX returns the first element of a group in response to the nonindexed notation, whereas BlueDragon returns the entire group as an array. Both platforms return NO if an element group is used as the argument for the IsArray() function.

The individual elements within a group can be addressed as though they were members in an array. So the organism element for bluefish in the example can be addressed as sealifeXML.sealife.fish.organism[1], and the organism element for shark can be addressed as sealifeXML.sealife.fish.organism[2]. At this point you may be asking, "But what if I want to get the organism for shark by asking for shark?" We'll look at that type of question a little later, when we talk about the XmlSearch function.

To get an element's text (the non-XML, non-comment content between its start and end tags), we use the designator XmlText appended to the element's reference. Thus, the reference sealifeXML.sealife.fish.XmlText returns the value **`Fish have gills.`**. Many XML vocabularies define data in a very simple "elements-only" style, with the name of a datapoint as the element and the value contained in the element's text.

Besides its text, an element can contain comments and other elements. The comments can be returned using the XmlComment designator, and the other elements are contained in the element's XmlChildren.

XmlComment returns only the comments within the element, i.e., those strings contained inside the comment symbols <!-- and -->. The reference sealifeXML.sealife.fish.XmlComment returns the value **`True for all fish?`**.

XmlChildren returns an array with one member for each element within the specified element (at the first sub-level only). If an element has no children, XmlChildren returns an empty array. An element's children only includes elements, not comments or text.

Elements are one of the two primary ways of encoding data in XML. The other way is attributes. We are all familiar with attributes within tags, as we use them all the time in HTML and CFML. They are just the name-value pairs found inside a starting tag. The next section deals with retrieving data from attributes.

Get an Attribute

In a CFML XML object, an element's attributes are contained within the designator XmlAttributes, which returns a structure. The reference `sealifeXML.sealife.fish.organism[2].XmlAttributes` returns the structure shown in Illustration 23.

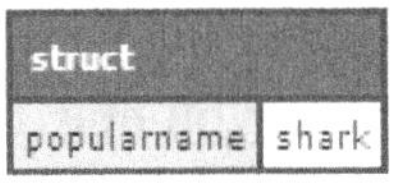

Illustration 23: XmlAttributes

The value of the popularname attribute can be retrieved with the reference `sealifeXML.sealife.fish.organism[2].XmlAttributes["popularname"]`. This would return the string **`shark`**. The simpler notation `sealifeXML.sealife.fish.organism[2].XmlAttributes.popularname` is also allowed.

> **CFMX vs. BlueDragon:** BlueDragon also allows the even simpler notation `sealifeXML.sealife.fish.organism[2].popularname` (eliminating the need for the XmlAttributes keyword). This notation will throw an error in CFMX.

Addressing datapoints in CFML XML objects is fairly straightforward. As with the previous chapter, though, there is another approach for extracting specific data from XML datasets in CFML. We used the XmlTransform() function to leverage XSLT for output of entire datasets. Now we'll look at using the XmlSearch() function with another standardized XML technology, XPath, to extract specific data.

XmlSearch() Function

The XmlSearch() function provides us with a way to directly extract data from an XML string. XmlSearch() uses search specifications that conform to the XPath standard.

> **NOTE:** XmlSearch() differs from the techniques we've seen so far, in that it operates on an XML string as well as a CFML XML object. There's no need to use XmlParse() or <CFXML> on an XML string prior to using XmlSearch().

The XmlSearch() function takes two arguments: the XML string from which we want to extract data, and an XPath-compliant string that specifies where to find the data. Let's look at a quick example from the sea life dataset. We want to find out the popularname of all the organisms inside the mollusks element.

```
result = XmlSearch(sealifeXML, "sealife/mollusks/organism/@popularname")
```

The result of the example is shown in Illustration 24. It is just an array of XML objects.

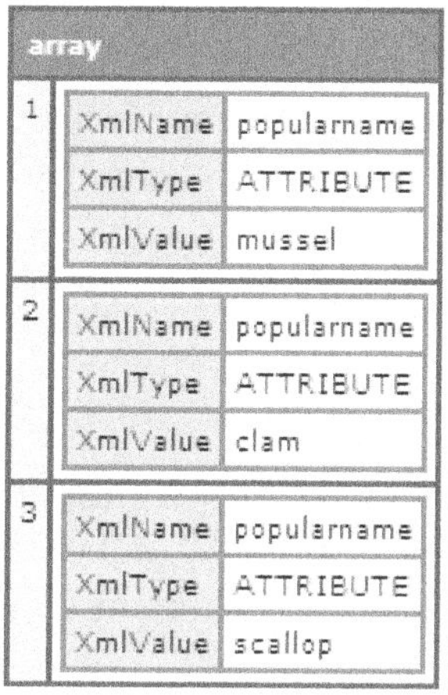

Illustration 24: XmlSearch() Result

To return each popularname, all we need to do is loop over the array and output the XmlValue for each member of the array:

```
<cfloop from="1" to="#ArrayLen(results)#" index="i">
  <cfoutput>#result[i].XmlValue#<br></cfoutput>
</cfloop>
```

The output from this code is the popularname of each element, each on its own line:

```
mussel
clam
scallop
```

In order to really take advantage of the XmlSearch() function, we need to know a little bit about XPath syntax. The next section deals with XPath and some of its basic features. Once you're comfortable with the basics, you can move on to explore more advanced features of XPath with a complete reference on XML and XPath. Note the CFMX does not support the complete XPath definition, so you might have to experiment a bit if you get around to using more complicated XPath expressions.

XPath

XPath is known formally as the XML Path Language. It is a standardized way to read data from an XML dataset. XPath includes a syntax for finding nodes like elements, attributes, and text; and a set of standard functions. The next few sections will give you an overview of some of the important features of XPath. For more information, there are plenty of XPath resources online. www.w3schools.com/xpath is a good place to start.

Find an element

One of the things we frequently want to do with XPath in the XmlSearch() function is to return a specific element. In XPath terminology, and element is a tag to CF developers. In other words, the <html> tag in an XHTML document would be referred to as an html element in XPath.

As you might have already guessed from the example we saw in the XmlSearch() function example, elements in XPath are expressed in terms of the XML data's hierarchy, with each level of the hierarchy represented by a slash (/). So in our sealife example, the mollusks element can be selected using the XPath

```
sealife/mollusks
```

If we use this XPath in the XmlSearch() function, like this:

```
results = XmlSearch(sealifeXML, 'sealife/mollusks')
```

the output stored in the variable results looks like the dump in Illustration 25.

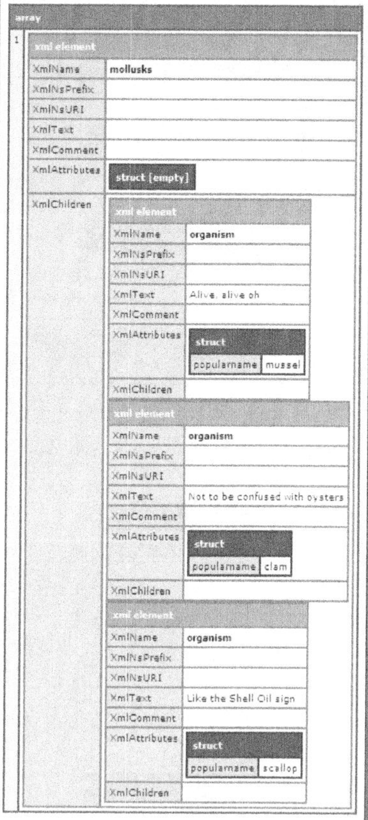

Illustration 25: XmlSearch for mollusks

This makes sense when there's only one element of the desired name, like our mollusks example. But what about situations where there are more than one? Let's take a look at the organism elements within the mollusks element for an answer. There are three distinct organisms within the mollusks category, so what happens if we make a request for the sealife/mollusks/organism element? Let's look at this example:

```
results = XmlSearch(sealifeXML, 'sealife/mollusks')
```

The output in the results variable is shown in Illustration 26.

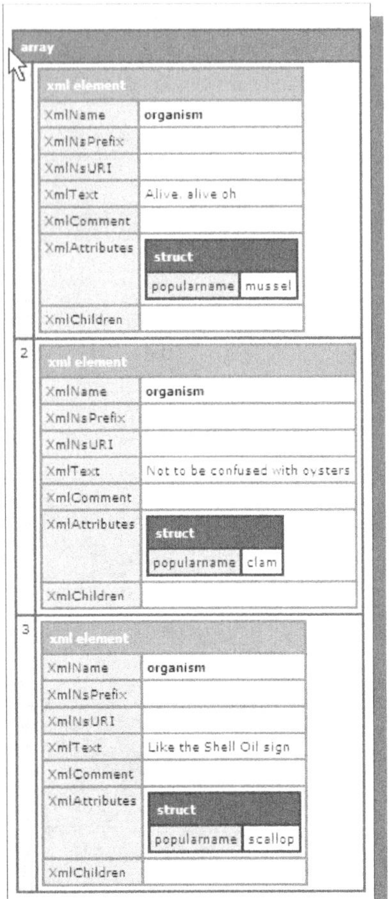

Illustration 26: XmlSearch for mollusks/organism

Note that the output from this search is identical to the content of the XmlChildren array from the previous example, shown in Illustration 25. This clearly shows the hierarchical relationships within the XML data, and how it is represented when returned by XmlSearch().

So now we know how to find elements according to the established hierarchy in our XML data. But what if we need find a set of elements the breaks the hierarchy? For example, what if we want all the organism elements in our dataset, regardless of which parent category they have? Fortunately, XPath gives us a way to do this as well. The double-slash (//) selector means “all the elements below this node that match the specified name”.

For example, let's use the XPath sealife//organism. What happens when we use it with the XmlSearch() function, like this:

```
results = XmlSearch(sealifeXML, 'sealife//organism')
```

First of all, notice that there are no **organism** nodes directly beneath the **sealife** node. This syntax says "all nodes below the sealife node that are organism nodes". The content of the results variable is shown in Illustration 27.

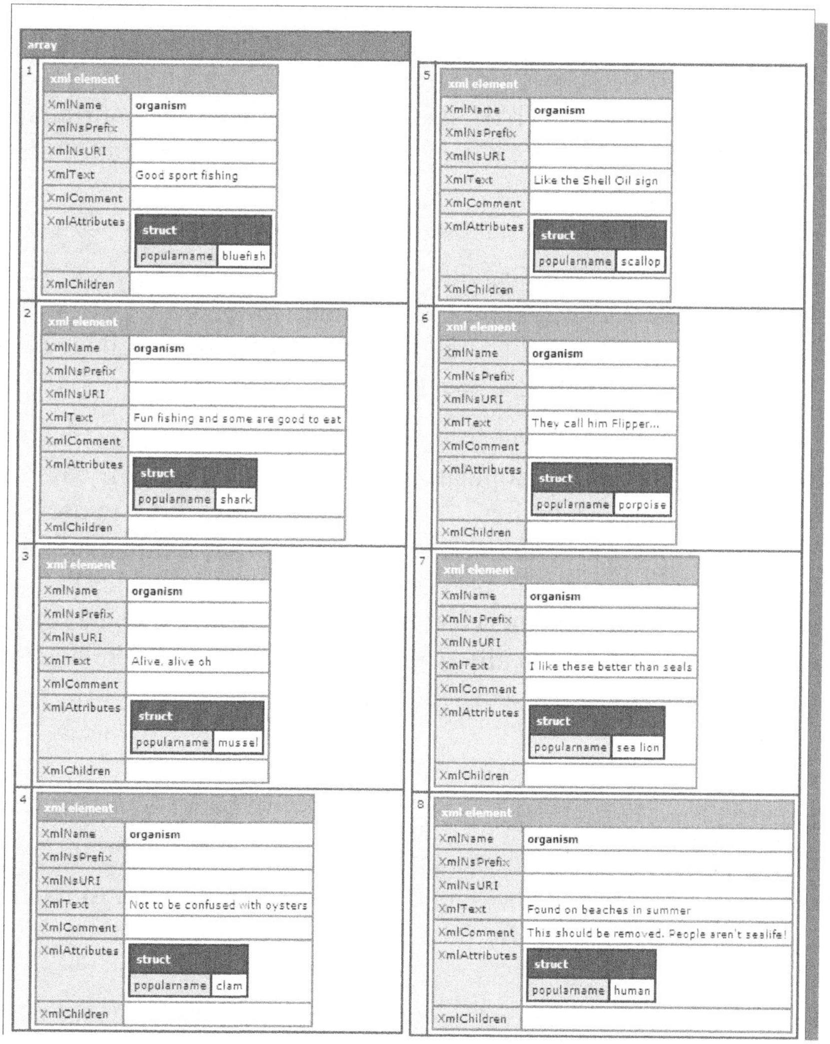

An important behavior of the double-slash selector is that it operates on every node below the node to the left of the selector. So this last example finds every **organism** below the **sealife** node. Because there are no **organism** nodes *above* the **sealife** node, we could also have used XmlSearch(sealifeXML,'//organism') to get the same result.

We are now able to use XPaths to return any element node we want from our XML dataset. But what if we want to return attribute nodes? There is important data contained in those attributes, after all. Let's take a look.

Find an Attribute

Just as the name-value pairs within HTML and CFML tags are called attributes, so they are also called attributes within XML. We'll sometimes refer to them as “attribute nodes”, particularly in the context of XPath.

In the first example we used for XmlSearch(), there is a use of the attribute selector. The attribute selector in XPath is the at symbol (@). So the syntax sealife/mollusks/organism/@popularname returns all the **popularname** attribute nodes for **organism** nodes under **mollusks** in **sealife**.

Now what if we want to fetch all the popularname attribute nodes in the dataset, just like we fetched all the organism nodes earlier? You might logically think to use the syntax @@popularname, since doubling the slash selector worked for element nodes. This logic is close, but not quite a cigar-winner. We need to remember that attributes belong to elements, so we need to use an element selector before using the attribute selector. To fetch all the popularname nodes, we really want to select all the element nodes that have the popularname attribute. So the correct syntax is //@popularname.

XPath Predicates

So far we've used XPath to select elements and attributes from the XML hierarchy without regard to their values. To further refine our selections, we might want to fetch nodes that meet specific criteria. This is the job for XPath predicates.

A predicate is simply a statement that refines a selection from the general to the specific, using one or more criteria. Predicates in XPath are surrounded by square brackets.

The simplest predicate is one that specifies a single instance in a collection of multiple elements. To illustrate this, we'll go back to the set of **organism** nodes under the **mollusks** node in our sealife dataset. Let's say we want to return just the first occurrence of an **organism** node. Here's the syntax:

```
result = XmlSearch(sealifeXML,"sealife/mollusks/organism[1]")
```

The result of this statement is shown in Illustration 28.

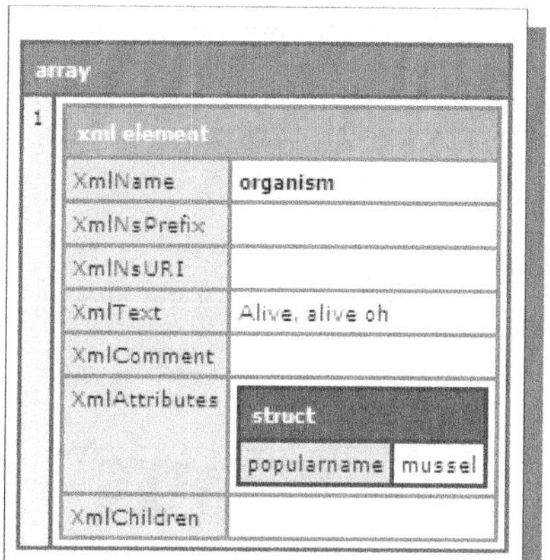

Illustration 28: XmlSearch of sealife/mollusks/organism[1]

As expected, we get the first occurrence of the organism element inside the mollusks element.

Predicates can also be used to evaluate the data contained in a node. For example, let's say we're aware of the anomaly in our data (the presence of a human), and we want to select all the mammals except that one. We can use a predicate to specify the criterion:

```
result = XmlSearch(sealifeXML,"sealife/mammals/organism[@popularname!='human']");
```

The result is shown in Illustration 29. We get back the two **organism** nodes that have a value for **popularname** other than "human".

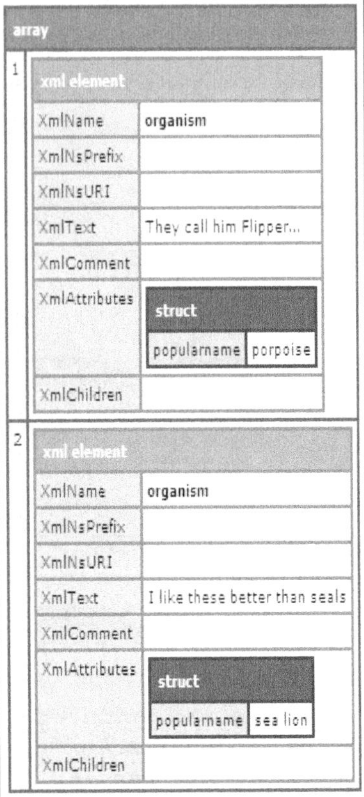

Illustration 29: XmlSearch for @popularname!='human'

Similarly, if we want to get just the **`popularname`** nodes for all non-human mammals, we can use this statement:

```
result = XmlSearch(sealifeXML,"sealife/mammals/organism[@popularname!='human']/popularname");
```

And the result from this refinement is shown in Illustration 30.

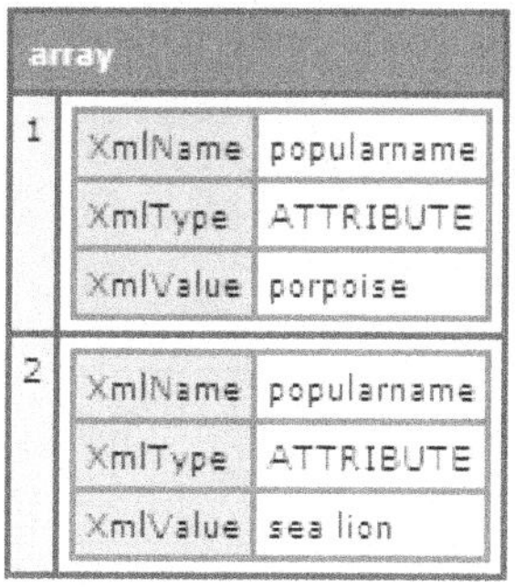

Illustration 30: XmlSearch for non-human popularnames

XPath Axes

An axis is another way to select nodes in the world of XPath. I like to think of axes as skewers: you can stick one into your dataset to pull out related nodes. There is an axis called *child;* it selects nodes that are children of the specified node. For example, we can select all children of the **`fish`** node with this statement:

```
result = XmlSearch(sealifeXML,"sealife/fish/child::*")
```

Illustration 31 shows the result of this statement.

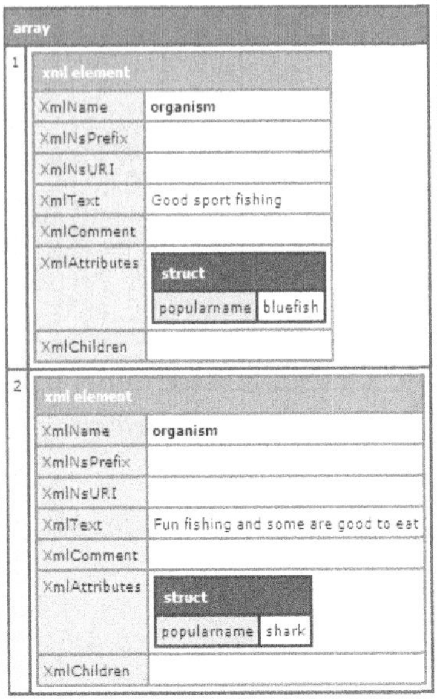

*Illustration 31: XmlSearch for sealife/fish/child::**

Axes can be very powerful selection tools. Let's take a look at the idea of selecting all organism nodes again. We're really asking for all **`organism`** nodes that are grandchildren of the **`sealife`** node. This can be expressed as "the organism nodes that are children of any of the children of sealife". In XPath syntax within the XmlSearch() function, that expression looks like this:

```
result = XmlSearch(sealifeXML,"sealife/child::*/organism")
```

The result is the same as when we used the expression `sealife//organism`, as shown in Illustration 27, but using the axis makes the intent much clearer. The difference between the two expressions becomes apparent when the dataset changes. What happens if our dataset has another **`organism`** node attached as a child to the **`organism`** node for *shark*? Here's the new data:

```
<sealife>
  <fish>Fish have gills.<!-- True for all fish? -->
    <organism popularname="bluefish">Good sport fishing</organism>
    <organism popularname="shark">Fun fishing and some are good to eat
      <organism type="symbiote" popularname="remora">
        Attaches to shark and rides along
      </organism>
    </organism>
  </fish>
  <mollusks>
    <organism popularname="mussel">Alive, alive oh</organism>
    <organism popularname="clam">Not to be confused with oysters</organism>
    <organism popularname="scallop">Like the Shell Oil sign</organism>
  </mollusks>
  <mammals>
    <organism popularname="porpoise">They call him Flipper...</organism>
    <organism popularname="sea lion">I like these better than seals</organism>
    <organism popularname="human">
      Found on beaches in summer
      <!-- This should be removed. People aren't sealife! -->
    </organism>
  </mammals>
</sealife>
```

Here's what happens if we use the XPath query from the earlier example, `sealife//organism`:

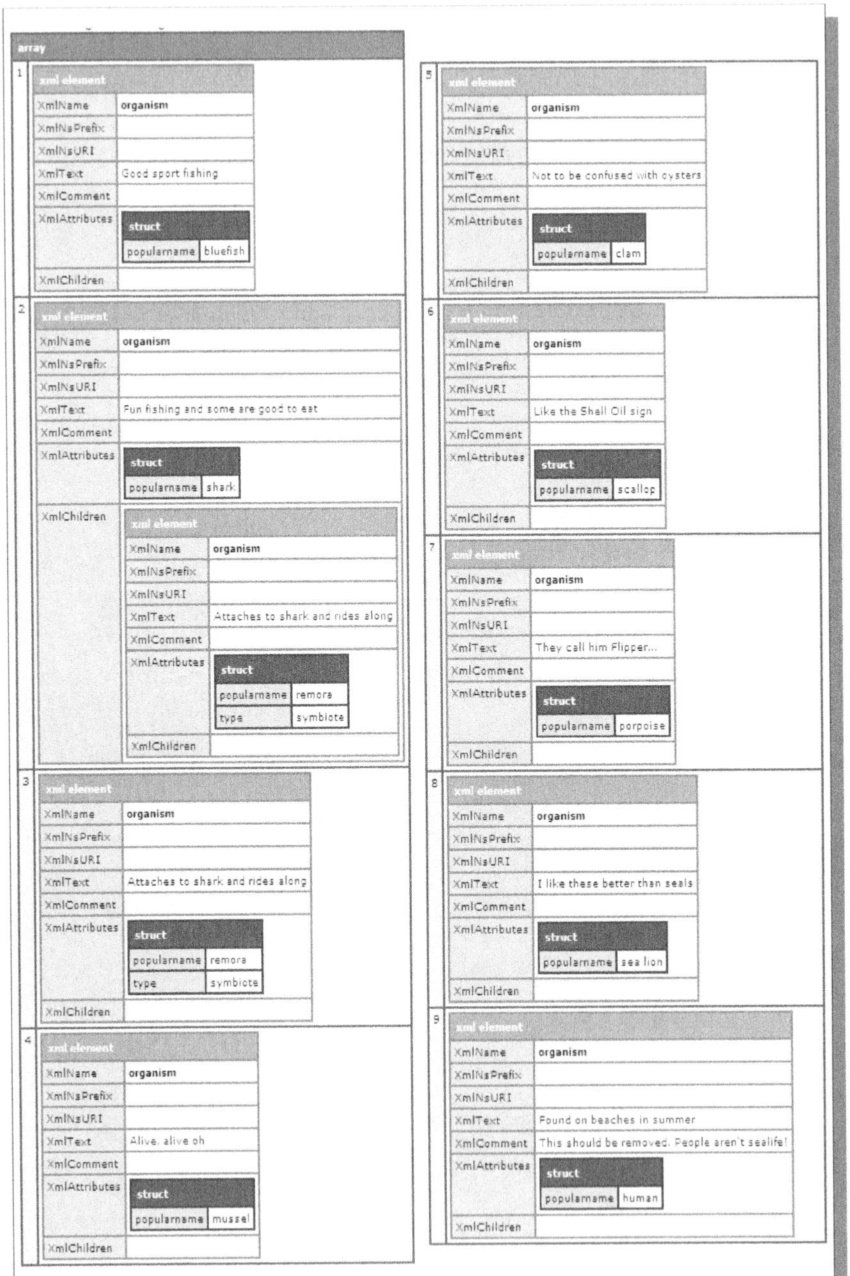

Illustration 32: XmlSearch for sealife//organism

Compare the result in Illustration 32 with the result in Illustration 33, which is what happens if we use the XPath query from the last example, `sealife/child::*/organism`:

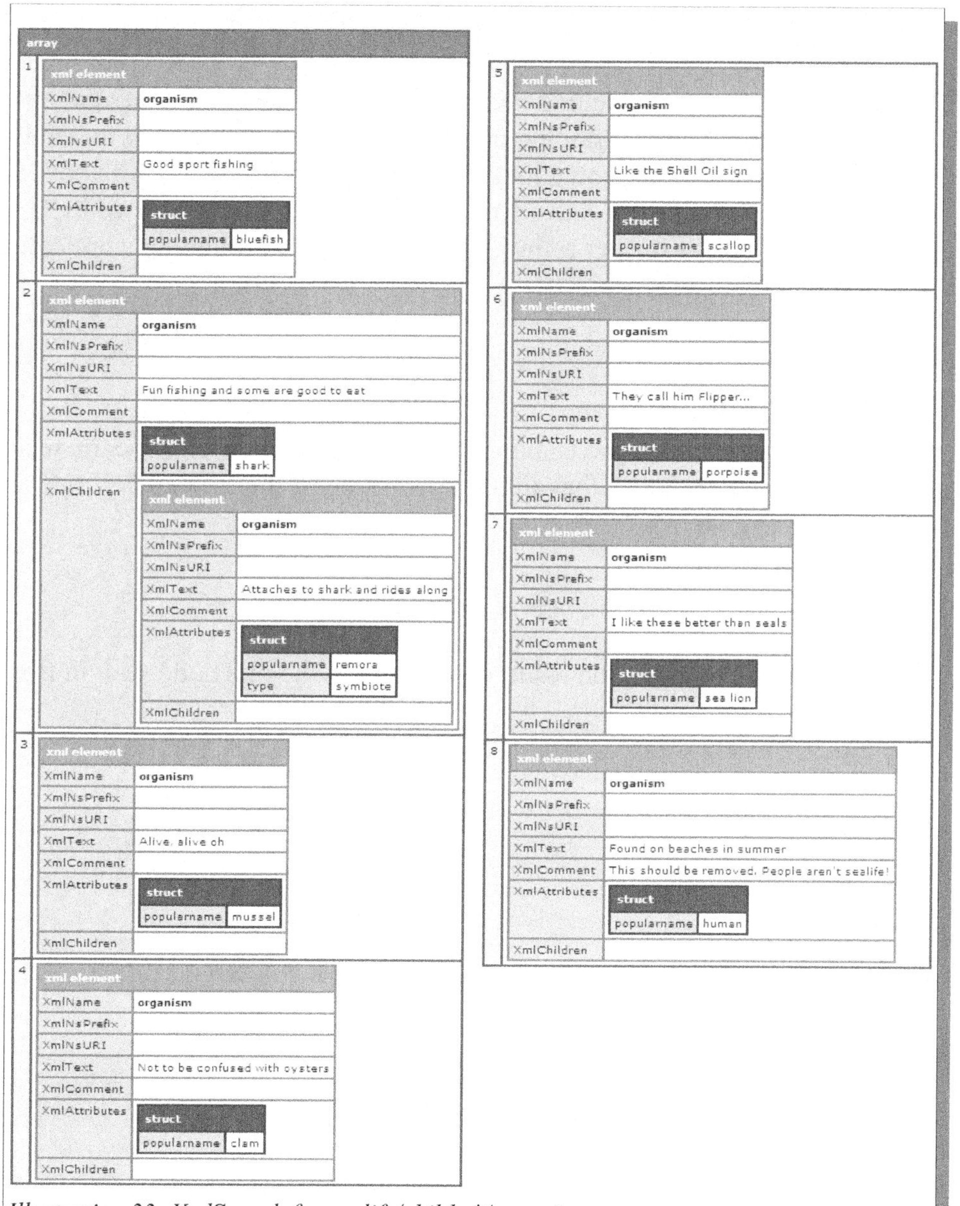

Illustration 33: XmlSearch for sealife/child::/organism*

The difference is indicated by the third member of each array. Where the first example (Illustration 32) has a member for the *remora* **`organism`**, the second example (Illustration 33) does not. Using the child axis ensures that the result contains only what we wanted: only the **`organism`** nodes that are grandchildren of the **`sealife`** node.

There are several other axes available in XPath, including *attribute*, *descendant*, and *ancestor*. All axes employ the same double-colon syntax we explored with the child axis, so a bit of experimentation will get you a long way. We won't go into detail about all the axes, since their names explain them fairly well and there is an axis reference in Appendix C. Instead, we'll take a look at further refining the use of axes through the application of predicates.

Predicates with XPath Axes

Just as with general node notation, we can apply predicates to axes to refine the results. Let's retrieve any **`organism`** nodes that are grandchildren of the **`sealife`** node and have a **`popularname`** value of *shark*:

```
result = XmlSearch(sealifeXML,"sealife/child::*/organism[@popularname='shark']")
```

As you probably expected by now, the result contains only the one node seen in Illustration 34.

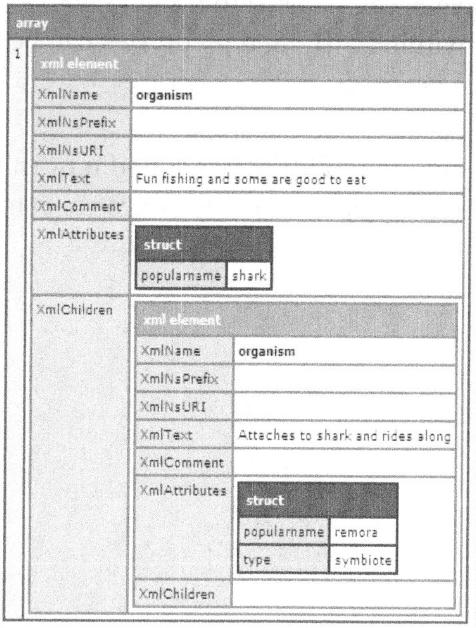

Illustration 34: XmlSearch for sealife/child::/organism[@popularname='shark']*

"But wait!" you're also saying, "The organism node for remora is in that result, too!"

Of course, you're right, but notice also that it is inside the XmlChildren part of the CF XML element for shark. When the XmlSearch() function returns a node, it includes that node's children in XmlChildren.

We now have a fairly good handle on how to pull data out of an XML dataset using XPath with the XmlSearch() function. There are many variations on the basic themes we've explored here, but they are beyond the scope of this book. Armed with the basic knowledge we have, and any search engine, we can explore the many nuances of XPath.

Summary

Data contained in XML can be extracted in a variety of ways using ColdFusion. We can directly address nodes within an XML object, or we can use the XmlSearch() function and XPath to extract desired chunks of data. XPath provides a very robust syntax for examining XML data. Predicates can be used to refine XPath expressions. Axes provide a way to address sets of nodes within XML, and predicates can be used in combination with them.

So we know how to get data out of an XML dataset, and how to address nodes within an XML object. Now let's turn our attention to other things we can do with XML-specific functions in CFML. That's the next chapter.

Chapter 6 - Other XML Functions in CFML

Introduction

In the last chapter, we spent quite a bit of time exploring the XmlSearch() function. While perhaps the most powerful XML-related function in CFML, it is certainly not the only one. This chapter provides an overview of other functions and examples for their use.

IsXmlDoc()

The XmlDoc() function takes one parameter: a variable to check for type. It returns **YES** if the variable is a CFML XML document, and **NO** if the variable is of any other type. When we need to check if a variable is an XML dataset (string) or a CFML XML document, this is the function to use. The following code illustrates it use:

```
<cffile action="read" file="e:\xmlData\sealife.xml" variable="seaLifeXML">
<cfdump var="#IsXmlDoc(seaLifeXML)#">  <!--- NO --->
<cfset seaLifeXmlDoc = XmlParse(seaLifeXML)>
<cfdump var="#IsXmlDoc(seaLifeXmlDoc)#">  <!--- YES --->
```

The output shows the difference between XML data in a string variable (seaLifeXML) and an XML data in a CFML XML document variable (seaLifeXmlDoc).

In what sort of scenario might we use the IsXmlDoc() function? Since the XmlSearch() function can operate on XML data strings and XML objects equally well, what's the point?

Certainly there are other ways we can manipulate and reference XML data than using the XmlSearch() function. For example, let's take a look at using dot notation. Here's some code with the sealife XML data stored in two different variables: sealifeXML and sealifeXMLDoc. Like the previous example, sealifeXML is an XML string, and sealifeXMLDoc is the same data in a CFML XML object. Let's see what happens when we try to get the text of the first fish organism node from the XML object:

```
<cfset myText = sealifeXMLDoc.sealife.fish.organism[1].XmlText>
<cfdump var="#myText#">
```

The result is the string **`Good sport fishing`**. What happens if we do the same thing using the sealifeXML variable instead?

```
<cfset myText = sealifeXML.sealife.fish.organism[1].XmlText>
<cfdump var="#myText#">
```

The result in this case is an error:

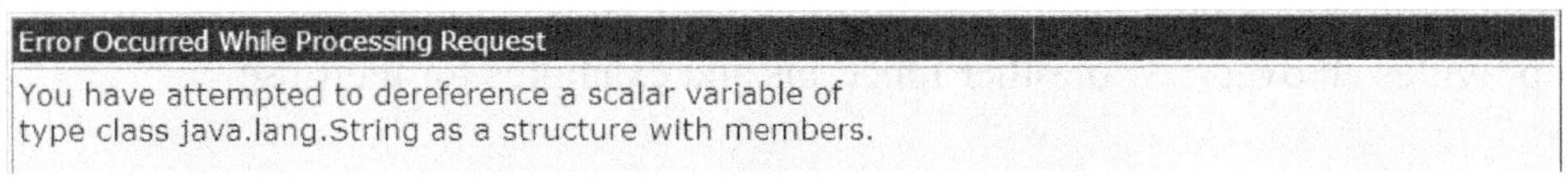

Illustration 35: Error From Dot-Notation Reference Against XML String

So we can't use dot notation to reference plain XML data. This is a case where we might want to test using IsXmlDoc() before we try to reference the data. If the test fails, we can use the IsXml() function to make sure the variable contains well-formed XML data (i.e., as a string), then the XmlParse() function can convert the data to an XML object.

There is also a function similar to IsXmlDoc() available for elements within an XML document.

IsXmlElem()

The IsXmlElem() function takes one argument. If the argument is an element in an XML object, the function returns **YES**; otherwise it returns **NO**. Here's an example to demonstrate, using the sealifeXMLDoc object:

```
<cfset myVar = sealifeXMLDoc.sealife.fish>
<cfdump var="#IsXmlElem(myVar)#">
```

The result of this code is YES, since there is an element in the XML that conforms to **<sealife><fish>**. We can even test to see if the node in question is the dataset's root node.

IsXmlRoot()

If you looked at the previous section on the IsXmlElem() function, you probably already know how IsXmlRoot() works. It takes one argument: a variable. It returns **YES** if the variable is the root element (root node) of a CFML XML object; otherwise it returns **NO**. Using our sealife dataset, `IsXmlRoot(seaLifeXmlDoc.sealife)` would return **YES**, while `IsXmlRoot(seaLifeXmlDoc.sealife.fish)` would return **NO**.

> **NOTE:** Every CFML XML object has a property named XmlRoot, which points to the root node of the object. So the expression `IsXmlRoot(myXMLObj.XmlRoot)` will always be true for an XML object named **myXMLObj**.

Here's an interesting point: what happens if the variable offered to IsXmlRoot() isn't even part of a CFML XML object? Let's give it a try:

```
<cfset myVar = “foo”>
<cfset result = IsXmlRoot(myVar)>
```

This bit of code returns **NO**, the same result we would get if the variable were a non-root element in an XML object. So the combination of IsXmlRoot() with IsXmlElem() can ensure that we're dealing with the expected data type. The following table enumerates the expected returns from this pair of functions.

Data Type	IsXmlElem()	IsXmlRoot()
XML object root node	YES	YES
XML object non-root node	YES	NO
Any other datatype	NO	NO

So we can readily identify whether a variable contains an XML element, and whether that element is the root of the XML object. Moving on, we can also identify whether a variable contains a node in an XML object.

IsXmlNode()

The IsXmlNode() function is very similar to the IsXmlElem() function, with an important difference. It takes one argument: a variable to evaluate. But where IsXmlElem() returns **NO** if the argument it is given is a CFML XML object, IsXmlNode() returns **YES**. So with the sealifeXmlDoc XML object, IsXmlElem(seaLifeXmlDoc) returns **NO**, and IsXmlNode(seaLifeXmlDoc) returns **YES**.

If you've worked with XML in environments other than CFML, you might be wondering about attributes in the XML object and their definition as nodes. Although attributes are indeed defined as nodes within the XML specification, ColdFusion does not treat them as such. Attributes and their values are always referenced through the XmlAttributes structure.

NOTE: BlueDragon 6.x does not have an IsXMLNode() function.

XmlChildPos()

The XmlChildPos() function returns the index of the specified child element of the specified parent element. It takes three arguments: a variable containing an XML element, the name of the child element array, and the index of the desired child element. If there is only one instance of the desired child element, the third argument will be 1.

Using the sealife example, we can return the index of the **mollusks** element in the **sealife** element with this code:

```
<cfset result = XmlChildPos(seaLifeXMLDoc.sealife, "mollusks",1)>
```

The result is **2**, indicating that the **mollusks** element is the second child of the **sealife** element.

Being able to determine the position of a particular child element allows us to modify or delete that element, in conjunction with the XmlChildren property of an element. The XmlChildren property is an array that contains all the child elements of the element in question.

Let's say we want to add some text inside the mollusks element. The following code allows us to do just that:

```
<cfset result = XmlChildPos(seaLifeXMLDoc.sealife, "mollusks",1)>
<cfset seaLifeXMLDoc.sealife.XmlChildren[result].XmlText = "Many mollusks are good eatin'!">
<cfdump var="#seaLifeXMLDoc.sealife.mollusks#">
```

A portion of the screen shot of the output is shown in Illustration 35. Note that the XmlText of the **mollusks** element has changed.

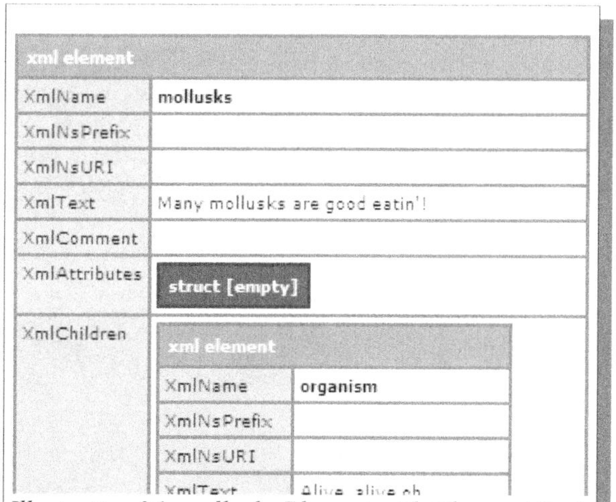

Illustration 36: mollusks Element with Changed Text

In terms of the text representation of this dataset, we can envision the altered **mollusks** element this way:

```
<mollusks>Many mollusks are good eatin'!
  <organism popularname="mussel">Alive, alive oh</organism>
  <organism popularname="clam">Not to be confused with oysters</organism>
  <organism popularname="scallop">Like the Shell Oil sign</organism>
</mollusks>
```

So we can easily inject new data into an XML object. But is it safe to just throw a string into the XmlText? What if the string arrives in the form of a variable, and we don't necessarily know what's in it? This is where the XmlFormat() function comes in.

XmlFormat()

The XmlFormat() function takes one argument: a string to convert into XML-compatible format. Just as the HTMLEditFormat() function converts a string into HTML-compatible encoding, the XmlFormat() function converts a string into a legal XML-compatible encoding.

Using the example from the previous section, let's change things so that the string we want to inject into the mollusks element is **`2006: mollusk population > human population`**. Clearly, the > symbol in this string would create a problem in an XML dataset. It needs to be properly encoded. Here's how we could approach the problem:

```
<cfset result = XmlChildPos(seaLifeXMLDoc.sealife, "mollusks",1)>
<cfset newText = "2006: mollusk population > human population">
<cfset seaLifeXMLDoc.sealife.XmlChildren[result].XmlText = XmlFormat(newText)>
<cfdump var="#seaLifeXMLDoc.sealife.mollusks#">
```

The output is shown in Illustration 36.

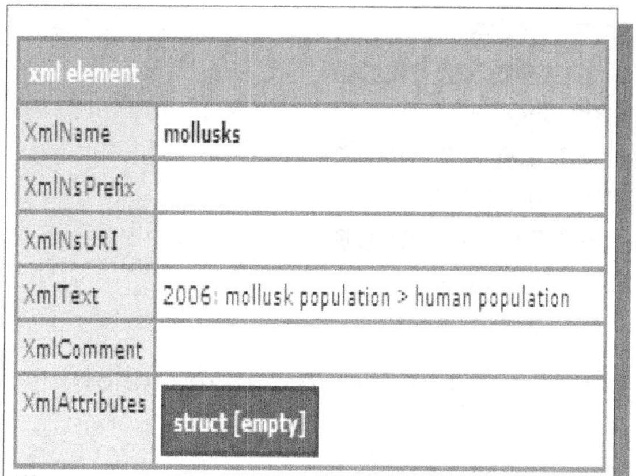

Illustration 37: mollusks with XmlFormat()ed text

Even though the XmlText in the screenshot looks just like the original text, we can see how it has been converted by looking at the immediate results of the XmlFormat() function: `<cfdump var="#XmlFormat(newText)#">` returns **`2006: mollusk population > human population`**. The **>** symbol has been changed to the XML-compatible **`>`**.

XmlGetNodeType()

An element in a CFML XML object has a property named XmlNodes. This attribute is an array that contains all the child nodes of the specified element. We can loop over this array and use the XmlGetNodeType() function to find out what the nodes are. The XmlGetNodeType() function takes one argument: a variable containing an element in an XML object. If the argument is not an element, the function throws an error.

Let's loop over the **`sealife.fish`** element's nodes in the sealife example and inspect the type of each node:

```
<cfset n = seaLifeXMLDoc.sealife.fish.XmlNodes>
<cfloop from="1" to="#ArrayLen(n)#" index="i">
  <cfoutput>
   #n[i].XmlName# has type #XMLGetNodeType(n[i])#<br />
  </cfoutput>
</cfloop>
```

The output shows each node's name and type:

```
#text has type TEXT_NODE
#comment has type COMMENT_NODE
#text has type TEXT_NODE
organism has type ELEMENT_NODE
#text has type TEXT_NODE
organism has type ELEMENT_NODE
#text has type TEXT_NODE
```

The XmlGetNodeType() function will return one of the following results:

```
ATTRIBUTE_NODE
CDATA_SECTION_NODE
COMMENT_NODE
DOCUMENT_FRAGMENT_NODE
DOCUMENT_NODE
DOCUMENT_TYPE_NODE
ELEMENT_NODE
ENTITY_NODE
ENTITY_REFERENCE_NODE
NOTATION_NODE
PROCESSING_INSTRUCTION_NODE
TEXT_NODE
```

Summary

To enhance its ability to manipulate XML data, CFML includes a collection of functions. This chapter addressed several of the functions that are not covered elsewhere in this book. These incude IsXmlDoc(), IsXml(), IsXmlElem(), IsXmlRoot(), IsXmlNode(), XmlChildPos(), XmlFormat(), and XmlGetNodeType(). Another XML function, IsWDDX(), opens the door to another world altogether. We'll take a look at it in the next chapter.

Chapter 7 - WDDX

What is WDDX?

Back in the early days of ColdFusion, the folks at Allaire saw a need to be able to exchange data between disparate environments. In particular, they wanted to be able to move complex datatypes from ColdFusion to Javascript and back. The solution they came up with is called Web Distributed Data eXchange (WDDX).

WDDX is an XML vocabulary. I'm sure this comes as no surprise to you by this point in the book. So let's take a peek at how to generate WDDX data, and then we'll see some examples on how to use it in applications.

How WDDX Works

WDDX is just a way to convert complex data into text. Since XML is such a great way to capture data, it makes sense that WDDX uses XML for exactly this purpose.

Let's take a look at how WDDX encodes two of the more popular CFML complex datatypes: arrays and structures. First, we'll build an array variable and a struture variable, and populate each with some data:

```
<cfscript>
 myArray = ArrayNew(1);
  myArray[1] = "Able";
  myArray[2] = "Baker";
  myArray[3] = "Charlie";

  myStruc = StructNew();
  myStruc.firstName = "Jeff";
  myStruc.lastName = "Peters";
</cfscript>

<cfdump var="#myArray#">
<cfdump var="#myStruc#">
```

The output from this bit of code is shown in Illustration 38. It's pretty standard fare for CF developers.

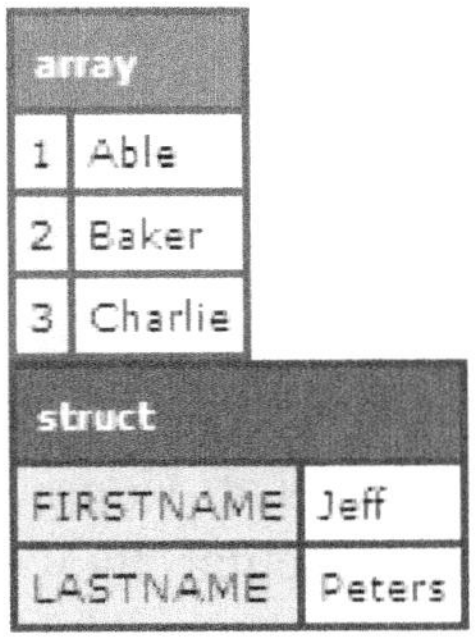

Illustration 38: Array and Structure

But what happens when we convert this data into WDDX? Here's some code to do just that:

```
<cfwddx action="cfml2wddx" input="#myArray#" output="myWDDXArray">
<cfwddx action="cfml2wddx" input="#myStruc#" output="myWDDXStruc">
```

The <CFWDDX> tag performs the conversion for us. If we CFDUMP the results to the screen, the output is really rather unimpressive, as seen in Illustration 39.

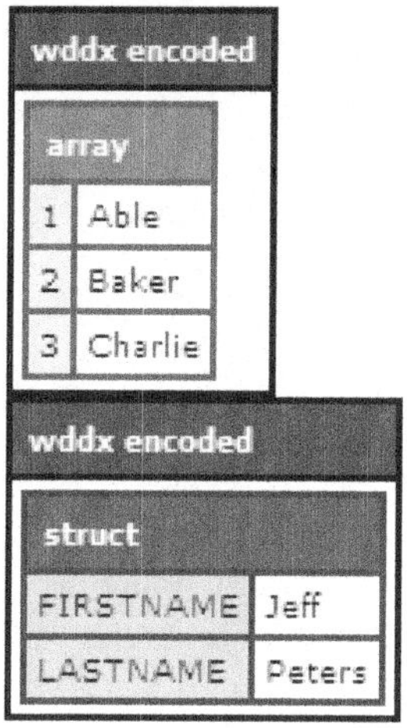

Illustration 39: WDDX Array and Structure

The CFDUMP output just puts a nicely formatted enclosure and title around each variable. To see what's really going on, we'll use CFOUTPUT and the HTMLCodeFormat() function to see the variables:

```
<cfoutput>
  #HTMLCodeFormat(myWDDXArray)#<br />
  #HTMLCodeFormat(myWDDXStruc)#
</cfoutput>
```

The output this time shows us something much more interesting:

```
<wddxPacket version='1.0'><header/><data><array
length='3'><string>Able</string><string>Baker</string><string>Charlie</string></array></dat
a></wddxPacket>
```

```
<wddxPacket version='1.0'><header/><data><struct><var
name='LASTNAME'><string>Peters</string></var><var
name='FIRSTNAME'><string>Jeff</string></var></struct></data></wddxPacket>
```

We begin to see a little bit better what's going on. For the sake of readability, let's tidy up the XML a little bit:

```
<wddxPacket version='1.0'>
  <header/>
  <data>
    <array length='3'>
```

```
      <string>Able</string>
      <string>Baker</string>
      <string>Charlie</string>
    </array>
  </data>
</wddxPacket>


<wddxPacket version='1.0'>
  <header/>
  <data>
    <struct>
      <var name='LASTNAME'>
        <string>Peters</string>
      </var>
      <var name='FIRSTNAME'>
        <string>Jeff</string>
      </var>
    </struct>
  </data>
</wddxPacket>
```

Aha! Now things are starting to lot like the XML we've been dealing with throughout this book. Pretty clever, no? We know that, if we so desire, we can apply any of the XML techniques we've learned to these pieces of data.

So if our system receives WDDX data from any source, we can do whatever we like with that data in addition to doing the typical actions that WDDX was designed to do. We can also check to see if some data is indeed valid WDDX.

The IsWDDX() Function

The IsWDDX() function takes one argument: a string. If the string is a valid WDDX data packet, the function returns **YES**; otherwise it returns **NO**. For example, if we use the myWDDXArray variable from the previous example, like this: IsWDDX(myWDDXArray), the result will be **YES**.

This function is useful in that it not only validates that a string is WDDX data, but also that it is well-formed. So if the string contains WDDX data but has something wrong with it in terms of well-formedness, the function will tell us so. To test this, let's introduce a mistake in the myWDDXArray variable. We'll misspell the end tag for the first string element, so the packet looks like this:

```
<wddxPacket version='1.0'>
```

```
  <header/>
  <data>
    <array length='3'>
      <string>Able</stirng>
      <string>Baker</string>
      <string>Charlie</string>
    </array>
  </data>
</wddxPacket>
```

When we try to output IsWDDX(myWDDXArray), we get **NO**. The error prevents the data from being well-formed WDDX.

Similarly, if we pass the IsWDDX() function a well-formed XML packet that isn't WDDX, we'll get **NO** as a result. So if we were to try IsWDDX(seaLifeXML), using the **seaLifeXML** variable from the previous chapter, we'd get **NO** as a result. The following table shows the possible results we can get from various values passed to IsWDDX().

Argument	IsWDDX(Argument) Returns
Well-formed WDDX packet (string)	**YES**
WDDX packet with a mistake (string)	**NO**
Well-formed non-WDDX XML packet (string)	**NO**
non-XML string	**NO**
any other datatype	**NO**

The <CFWDDX> tag gives us the ability to create WDDX packets for interchange with other systems. But it also gives us the ability to directly convert from CFML complex data to Javascript complex data.

CFML to Javascript

There are many solutions for which we might want to convert CF complex data into its Javascript analog. One of the most common of these is using a CF-generated array to insert data into an HTML page using Javascript—an approach popularized by the Ajax movement.

For example, we might have three different CF arrays. We want to use one of the arrays' values to populate a droplist control, depending on some other action on the page. The array to use will change depending on the user's action.

To prepare for this, we take the three CF arrays and make them available in Javascript by using the <CFWDDX> tag with the CFML2JS action:

```
<cfwddx action="cfml2js" input="#myArray1#" toplevelvariable="myJSArray1">
<cfwddx action="cfml2js" input="#myArray2#" toplevelvariable="myJSArray2">
<cfwddx action="cfml2js" input="#myArray3#" toplevelvariable="myJSArray3">
```

The toplevelvariable attribute specifies the name of the Javascript array to be created. When the CF template is rendered, the <CFWWDX> tag for the first line generates this Javascript:

```
myJSArray1 =  new Array();
myJSArray1[0] = "Able";
myJSArray1[1] = "Baker";
myJSArray1[2] = "Charlie";
```

Each line generates similar Javascript for its array. Note that the <CFWDDX> tag does NOT generate <SCRIPT> tags. Our CF template will need to surround the <CFWDDX> tags with <SCRIPT> tags to enable the Javascript.

Now the CF arrays have been converted to Javascript arrays, and we can work with them using Javascript.

Javascript to WDDX

Going back the other direction, we might want to use Javascript data in our CFML applicaiton as well. For example, we might want to use a Javascript-generated array in a CFML action page. In this case, we need some help on the Javascript end to create WDDX data. This help comes in the form of the wddx.js Javascript library.

To do the inverse of the array conversion above, we first include the wddx.js library, then convert the array. Conversion of data from its native form to WDDX is called serialization, so the Javascript process uses an object called WddxSerializer.

```
<script type="text/javascript" src="/CFIDE/scripts/wddx.js"></script>

<script>
    ws = new WddxSerializer();
    wddxData = ws.serialize(myArray);
</script>
```

The resulting WDDX packet can then be sent to a CFML action page by assigning its value to a form field and submitting the form:

```
<form name="myForm">
  <input type="hidden" name="wddxArray" />
</form>

<script>
   myForm.action = 'aCFMLActionPage.cfm';
   myForm.wddxArray.value = wddxData;
   myForm.submit();
</script>
```

In the action page aCFMLActionPage.cfm, we would use the <CFWDDX> tag with the WDDX2CFML action to deserialize the WDDX packet into a CFML array.

Summary

WDDX is an XML-based means of encoding complex data. It allows datatypes like arrays, structures, and recordsets to be exchanged between disparate environments. In CFML, we use the <CFWDDX> tag to convert complex data to WDDX packets. In Javascript, the wddx.js library provides similar functionality. The process of converting native data to a WDDX packet is called serialization; the inverse process is called deserialization. More information on WDDX can be found at the OpenWDDX.org website.

Chapter 8 - XML and Fusebox

Introduction

The bulk of this book has dealt with the use of XML in CFML applications from a fairly theoretical perspective. The example datasets are rather fanciful and don't offer a great deal of insight into the power of XML in real-world applications. This chapter is where that all changes.

Fusebox is, by most counts, the most popular framework for developing CFML applications. As of Fusebox 4, XML became a major part of the Fusebox specification. XML vocabularies are used for the application and circuit configuration files. In addition, the Fusedoc standard for documenting individual code templates is also an XML vocabulary. Knowing this, we can mine and leverage a great deal of information about Fusebox 4 applications.

Application Configuration

Every Fusebox 4 application has one application configuration file, named fusebox.xml. It is frequently seen with a .cfm extension added (fusebox.xml.cfm) to prevent inadvertent browsing of the file's contents.

The application configuration file sets up the basic Fusebox framework for the entire application. It sections are circuits, classes, parameters, globalfuseactions, and plugins. Each section is expressed as an XML element, and contains subelements pertinent to that section. The following code is the application configuration file for the basic version of the Fusebox reference application, Wegot Widgets.

```xml
<?xml version="1.0" encoding="UTF-8"?>
<fusebox>
   <circuits>
      <circuit alias="admin" path="admin/" />
      <circuit alias="browse" path="browse/" />
      <circuit alias="catalog" path="" />
   </circuits>

   <classes>
   </classes>

   <parameters>
      <parameter name="fuseactionVariable" value="fuseaction" />
      <parameter name="defaultFuseaction" value="browse.showCatalog" />
      <parameter name="precedenceFormOrUrl" value="form"/>
      <parameter name="mode" value="development"/>
      <parameter name="password" value=""/>
      <parameter name="parseWithComments" value="true" />
      <parameter name="conditionalParse" value="false" />
      <parameter name="ignoreBadGrammar" value="false"/>
      <parameter name="useAssertions" value="true" />
      <parameter name="scriptlanguage" value="cfmx" />
      <parameter name="scriptFileDelimiter" value="cfm"/>
      <parameter name="maskedFileDelimiters" value="htm,cfm,cfml,php,php4,asp,aspx"/>
      <parameter name="characterEncoding" value="utf-8"/>
   </parameters>

   <globalfuseactions>
      <preprocess>
         <do action="catalog.header" />
      </preprocess>
      <postprocess>
         <do action="catalog.footer" />
      </postprocess>
   </globalfuseactions>

   <plugins>
      <phase name="preProcess">
      </phase>
      <phase name="preFuseaction">
      </phase>
      <phase name="postFuseaction">
      </phase>
      <phase name="fuseactionException">
      </phase>
      <phase name="postProcess">
      </phase>
      <phase name="processError">
      </phase>
   </plugins>
```

```
</fusebox>
```

While this is not a book on Fusebox, we can take a couple of minutes to review the purpose of these configuration files. Most of the purposes of the elements within the fusebox.xml file can be inferred from their names, so we won't discuss their particulars. For in-depth information on Fusebox, see my books *Fusebox 4: Master-Class ColdFusion Applications* and *What's New in Fusebox 4.1*, both from Proton Arts.

Just as the fusebox.xml file is responsible for overall application configuration, circuit.xml files are responsible for the configuration of individual circuits.

Circuit Configuration

Within each circuit directory of a Fusebox 4 application is a circuit configuration file, named circuit.xml. As with the application configuration file, a .cfm extension is often appended (circuit.xml.cfm) to prevent unwanted browsing.

A circuit configuration file defines the fuseactions that are available to the application, and the fuses (templates) and/or actions that each fuseaction uses. The following code is one of the circuit configuration files from the basic version of the Fusebox reference application, Wegot Widgets.

```
<circuit access="public">
   <fuseaction name="showCatalog">
      <xfa name="lnkProductName" value="browse.showProduct" />
      <xfa name="lnkAdmin" value="Admin.showNewProductForm" />
      <include template="qryGetCatalog" />
      <include template="dspCatalog"/>
   </fuseaction>

   <fuseaction name="showProduct">
     <xfa name="lnkBackToCatalog" value="browse.showCatalog" />
     <include template="qryGetProduct" />
       <include template="dspProduct" />
   </fuseaction>
</circuit>
```

One of the most useful characteristics of circuit configuration files is their "roadmap" nature. We can easily understand the purpose of each fuseaction, and the flow of the application, by looking at each fuseaction, its contents, and its exit fuseactions (<xfa> elements). This aspect will become increasingly important later in the chapter when we look at leveraging the XML. Before that, though, let's take a quick look at one more XML vocabulary often seen in Fusebox applications.

Fusedoc

Although not required by Fusebox, Fusedoc-based comments are frequently seen in Fusebox applications. We can also take advantage of their power in non-Fusebox applications.

A Fusedoc is just a structured comment block at the top of a fuse (template). It defines responsibilities, properties, and IO for the template. In the Fusebox Lifecycle Process (FLiP), Fusedocs are actually written before the code, becoming a blueprint for the coder to follow.

The following code is a Fusedoc from one of the fuses in the basic version of the Fusebox reference application, Wegot Widgets.

```
<!---
<fusedoc fuse="dspCatalog.cfm" version="2.0" language="ColdFusion">
  <responsibilities>
    I display the current catalog listing.
  </responsibilities>
  <properties>
    <history type="create" email="jeff@grokfusebox.com" />
  </properties>
  <io>
    <in>
      <string name="xfa.lnkProductName" />
      <string name="xfa.lnkAdmin" />
      <recordset name="qryGetCatalog">
            <number name="productID" precision="integer" />
            <string name="productName" />
            <string name="productDescription" />
            <string name="imageFile" />
            <number name="price" />
          </recordset>
        </in>
        <out>
          <number name="productID" oncondition="XFA.lnkProductName" />
        </out>
    </io>
</fusedoc>
 --->
```

So we've taken a quick look at how the application configuration, circuit configurations, and fuses in a Fusebox 4 application use XML. Now we can consider how all that structured data might become a very powerful tool for us.

Leverage the Power

Within a Fusebox 4 application, the XML-based configuration files already play a powerful role. They are used by the Fusebox core files to control the application configuration and program flow of the application. This means that a Fusebox 4 application can be moved from a CFML environment to a different environment—PHP for example---and the only thing that has to be recoded is the actual fuses. The application configuration and program flow, encoded in XML, remain untouched.

Stepping back a bit, the fact that all this information is encoded in XML provides enormous opportunities for the management of the application development process, and documentation of the finished product.

What if we could have a checklist of all the templates that need to be coded for an application, automatically handed to us before coding starts? What if we could have printed documentation for every template in the application automatically created for us? What if we could have a map of the application's architecture automatically produced for us? Let's take a look at how the techniques we've already learned in this book make all these things possible.

Recursion and XSLT

Let's start with the idea of a checklist of all templates that need to be coded. We've seen that we have references to all the templates used in an application in the circuit.xml files. Each circuit template (fuse) is specified in an <include> element.

So all we need to provide our automated checklist is a utility that will combine some recursion and a little XSLT to build the checklist. We need the recursion to cause the utility to run itself for each directory in the application, and we need the XSLT transformation to transform each circuit.xml dataset into a checklist. This is exactly what the FB4Checklister utility does.

FB4Checklister

FB4Checklister is a free utility you can download from GrokFusebox.com. Called as a custom tag, it reads any circuit.xml files in the specified directory and any subdirectories, and applies the specified XSL stylesheet to the data. The collected results are presented to the browser for printing.

The following code shows the default stylesheet used with FB4Checklister.

```
<?xml version='1.0'?>
<xsl:stylesheet version="1.0" xmlns:xsl="http://www.w3.org/1999/XSL/Transform">
<xsl:output method="html" doctype-public="-//W3C//DTD HTML 4.0 Transitional//EN" />

<xsl:template match="/">
 <html>
  <head>
   <title>Fusebox Project Management Checklist</title>
   <style>
    th { font-family: Arial, Helvetica, sans-serif;
          font-size: 8pt;
         font-weight: 700; }
     td { font-family: Arial, Helvetica, sans-serif;
          font-size: 8pt;
         font-weight: 400; }
   </style>
  </head>
  <body>
   <div align="center"
      style="font-family: Arial;
          font-weight: 700;
            font-size: 14pt;">
   Fusebox Circuit Checklist - @@@[Circuit Directory]
   </div>
   <xsl:apply-templates select="circuit" />
   <br style="page-break-after:always;" />
  </body>
 </html>
</xsl:template>

<xsl:template match="circuit">
 <table border="1" align="center" width="100%">
  <xsl:apply-templates select="fuseaction" />
 </table>
</xsl:template>

<xsl:template match="fuseaction">
 <tr bgcolor="#e0e0e0">
  <th width="10">
   _
  </th>
  <th align="left" colspan="5">
   Fuseaction: <xsl:value-of select="@name" />
  </th>
 </tr>
 <tr>
  <th align="left" colspan="2">
   Fuse Name
  </th>
  <th align="left">
   Date Coded
```

```
    </th>
    <th align="left">
      Coded By
    </th>
    <th align="left">
      Unit Test Date
    </th>
    <th align="left">
      Tested By
    </th>
  </tr>
  <xsl:apply-templates select="include" />
</xsl:template>

<xsl:template match="include">
  <tr>
    <th width="10">

    _
    </th>
    <td align="left">
      <xsl:value-of select="@template" />
    </td>
    <td align="left">
      |
    </td>
    <td align="left">
      |
    </td>
    <td align="left">
      |
    </td>
    <td align="left">
      |
    </td>
  </tr>
</xsl:template>

</xsl:stylesheet>
```

The result of running FB4Checklister with the default XSL stylesheet is shown in Illustration 40.

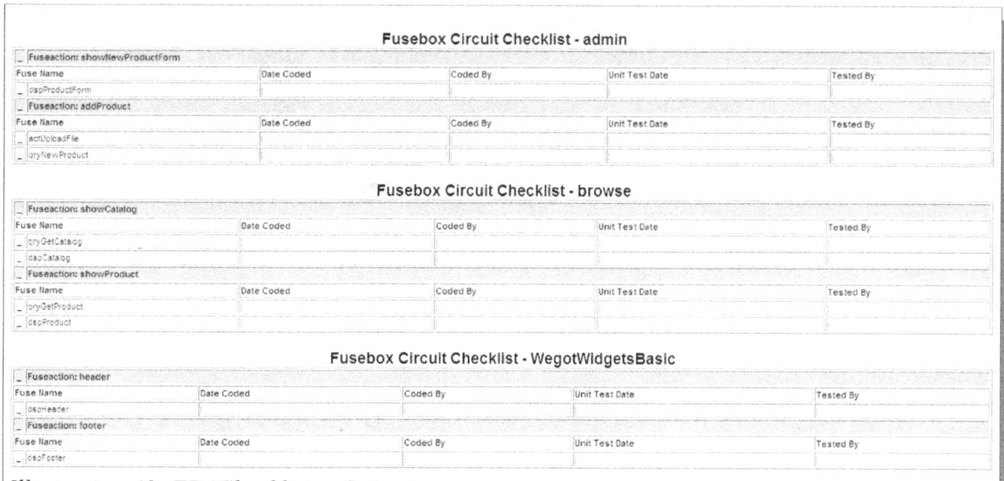

Fusebox Circuit Checklist - admin

Fuseaction: showNewProductForm				
Fuse Name	Date Coded	Coded By	Unit Test Date	Tested By
dspProductForm				

Fuseaction: addProduct				
Fuse Name	Date Coded	Coded By	Unit Test Date	Tested By
actUploadFile				
qryNewProduct				

Fusebox Circuit Checklist - browse

Fuseaction: showCatalog				
Fuse Name	Date Coded	Coded By	Unit Test Date	Tested By
qryGetCatalog				
dspCatalog				

Fuseaction: showProduct				
Fuse Name	Date Coded	Coded By	Unit Test Date	Tested By
qryGetProduct				
dspProduct				

Fusebox Circuit Checklist - WegotWidgetsBasic

Fuseaction: header				
Fuse Name	Date Coded	Coded By	Unit Test Date	Tested By
dspHeader				

Fuseaction: footer				
Fuse Name	Date Coded	Coded By	Unit Test Date	Tested By
dspFooter				

Illustration 40: FB4Checklister Output

Of course, the real power of XSLT is that we can apply a completely different stylesheet to get a completely different result. Because FB4Checklister allows us to specify the stylesheet, we can cause it to perform another task on the list we specified above.

Other XSL Stylesheets

By creating a new stylesheet, as shown in the following code segment, we can produce an outline of the application. This outline file, when imported into a diagramming tool called MindMapper, produces the graphical representation of the application shown in Illustration 41 (in this case, the Wegot Widgets Basic application).

```
<?xml version='1.0'?>
<xsl:stylesheet version="1.0" xmlns:xsl="http://www.w3.org/1999/XSL/Transform">
<xsl:output method="text" />

<xsl:template match="/">
 <xsl:apply-templates select="circuit" />
</xsl:template>

<xsl:template match="circuit">
 ct:@@@[Circuit Directory]<xsl:apply-templates select="fuseaction" />
</xsl:template>

<xsl:template match="fuseaction">
   fa:<xsl:value-of select="@name" />
   <xsl:apply-templates select="include" />
   <xsl:apply-templates select="xfa" />
</xsl:template>

<xsl:template match="include">
     ff:<xsl:value-of select="@template" />
</xsl:template>

<xsl:template match="xfa">
       xfa:<xsl:value-of select="@name" />=<xsl:value-of select="@value" />
</xsl:template>

</xsl:stylesheet>
```

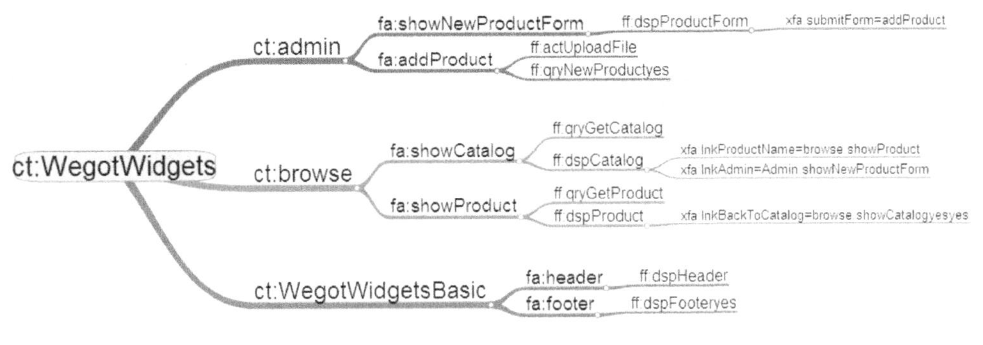

Illustration 41: Mindmap of Wegot Widgets Basic

Extending the Concept

The previous example shows that we can very easily take advantage of the XML data contained in a Fusebox 4 application. Based on the simple FB4Checklister engine, we can produce any kind of output based on the data in the application's circuit.xml files.

Extending this concept, we could perform similar operations on the other XML vocabularies in the application. We might use the data in the fusebox.xml file to produce an overview report on the application. Or we could write a utility to use the Fusedoc in each fuse file to create technical documentation for the system. Let's see what that would look like.

First, we'd need to modify the FB4Checklister.cfm module to read fuse files instead of circuit.xml files. Let's call it FusedocMiner.cfm. The code is shown below.

```
<!---
<fusedoc fuse="FusedocMiner.cfm" language="ColdFusion" version="2.0">
 <responsibilites>
  I read a Fusebox 4 application's fuse files, starting at the current directory,
  and produce an XSLT transformation from the specified stylesheet.
 </responsibilities>
 <properties>
  <history date="21 Feb 2006" author="Jeff Peters" email="jeff@grokfusebox.com" type="create">
   Version 1.0
  </history>
 </properties>
 <io>
  <in>
   <string name="thisDir" scope="attributes" optional="true" default="current path" />
   <boolean name="recurse" scope="attributes" optional="true" default="yes" />
   <string name="xslFile" optional="true" default="FusedocMiner.xsl" />
  </in>
  <out>
  </out>
 </io>
</fusedoc>
--->
<cfparam name="attributes.thisDir"
default="#GetDirectoryFromPath(GetCurrentTemplatePath())#">
<cfparam name="attributes.recurse" default="yes">
<cfparam name="attributes.xslFile" default="#attributes.thisDir#\FusedocMiner.xsl">
<cfparam name="attributes.fusePrefixes" default="dsp,act,qry">
<cfparam name="attributes.outputFile" default="#attributes.thisDir#FusedocMinerOutput.html">

<!--- Read directory entries into array --->
<cfdirectory name="qryThisDir"
        action="LIST"
      directory="#attributes.thisDir#">

<!--- For each entry in files array: --->
<cfloop query="qryThisDir">
 <!--- Select based on entry type: --->
 <cfswitch expression="#Trim(qryThisDir.type)#">
  <cfcase value="File">
   <!--- If it's a fuse file, transform it and write it to the output file --->

   <cfif ListFindNoCase(attributes.fusePrefixes,Left(qryThisDir.Name,3))>
    <cfset dirName = ListLast(attributes.thisDir,"\")>
    <cffile action="read"
           file="#attributes.thisDir#\#qryThisDir.Name#"
        variable="fuseFile">
         <!--- Strip out the Fusedoc --->
         <cfset inFusedoc = false>
         <cfset fusedocText = "">
         <cfloop from="1" to="#ListLen(fuseFile,Chr(10))#" index="i">
            <cfif FindNoCase("<fusedoc",ListGetAt(fuseFile,i,Chr(10)))>
```

```
                <cfset inFusedoc = true>
            </cfif>
            <cfif inFusedoc>
                <cfset fusedocText = fusedocText & ListGetAt(fuseFile,i,Chr(10))>
            </cfif>
            <cfif FindNoCase("</fusedoc",ListGetAt(fuseFile,i,Chr(10)))>
                <cfset inFusedoc = false>
            </cfif>
          </cfloop>
        <cffile action="read"
                file="#attributes.xslFile#"
              variable="xslCode">
      <cfset newHTML = XMLTransform(fusedocText, xslCode)>
          <cffile action="append"
                  file="#attributes.outputFile#"
                  output="#newHTML#"
             addnewline="true">
    </cfif>
  </cfcase>

  <cfcase value="Dir">
    Reading <cfoutput>#qryThisDir.Name#</cfoutput><br />
    <!--- Prevent recursion of the entire hard drive --->
    <cfif not ListFind(".,..",qryThisDir.Name) AND attributes.recurse>
      <!--- If directory entry, recurse with main   --->
      <cf_FusedocMiner thisDir="#attributes.thisDir#\#qryThisDir.Name#"
                  recurse="#attributes.recurse#"
                  xslFile="#attributes.xslFile#"
              fusePrefixes="#attributes.fusePrefixes#"
               outputFile="#attributes.outputFile#">
    </cfif>
  </cfcase>
  <cfdefaultcase>
    No handler for #qryThisDir.type#.
  </cfdefaultcase>
 </cfswitch>
</cfloop>
```

Then we need to create a stylesheet to transform a Fusedoc. One possibility is shown below, and the output it creates for a single Fusedoc is shown in Illustration 42.

```
<?xml version='1.0'?>
<xsl:stylesheet version="1.0" xmlns:xsl="http://www.w3.org/1999/XSL/Transform">
<xsl:output method="html" doctype-public="-//W3C//DTD HTML 4.0 Transitional//EN" />

<xsl:template match="/">
 <html>
  <head>
   <title>Fusebox Application Fuse Documentation</title>
   <link href="fusedocMiner.css" rel="stylesheet" type="text/css" />
  </head>
  <body>
  <div align="left"
     style="font-family: Arial;
          font-weight: 700;
            font-size: 14pt;">
   Fusebox Application Fuse Documentation
  </div>
   <xsl:apply-templates select="fusedoc" />
   <br style="page-break-after:always;" />
  </body>
 </html>
</xsl:template>

<xsl:template match="fusedoc">
  <span id="fuseName"><xsl:value-of select="@fuse" /></span>
  <xsl:apply-templates select="responsibilities" />
  <xsl:apply-templates select="properties" />
  <xsl:apply-templates select="io" />
</xsl:template>

<xsl:template match="responsibilities">
 <table class="responsibilitiesTable">
  <tr>
   <th>Responsibilities</th>
  </tr>
  <tr>
   <td><xsl:apply-templates select="text()" /></td>
  </tr>
 </table>
</xsl:template>

<xsl:template match="properties">
 <table class="propertiesTable">
  <tr>
   <th colspan="7">Properties</th>
  </tr>
   <xsl:apply-templates select="property" />
   <xsl:apply-templates select="history" />
   <xsl:apply-templates select="note" />
 </table>
</xsl:template>
```

```
<xsl:template match="property">
  <tr>
    <td>Property: <xsl:value-of select="@name" /></td>
    <td>Value: <xsl:value-of select="@value" /></td>
    <td colspan="2">Comments: <xsl:value-of select="@comments" /></td>
    <td colspan="3"><xsl:apply-templates select="text()" /></td>
  </tr>
</xsl:template>

<xsl:template match="history">
  <tr>
    <td>History Date: <xsl:value-of select="@date" /></td>
    <td>Author: <xsl:value-of select="@author" /></td>
    <td>Email: <xsl:value-of select="@email" /></td>
    <td>Role: <xsl:value-of select="@role" /></td>
    <td>Type: <xsl:value-of select="@type" /></td>
    <td>Comments: <xsl:value-of select="@comments" /></td>
    <td><xsl:apply-templates select="text()" /></td>
  </tr>
</xsl:template>

<xsl:template match="note">
  <tr>
    <td>Note Date: <xsl:value-of select="@date" /></td>
    <td>Author: <xsl:value-of select="@author" /></td>
    <td colspan="5"><xsl:apply-templates select="text()" /></td>
  </tr>
</xsl:template>

<xsl:template match="text()">
  <xsl:value-of select="."/>
</xsl:template>

<xsl:template match="io">
  <table class="ioTable">
    <tr>
      <th colspan="9">I/O</th>
    </tr>
      <xsl:apply-templates select="in" />
      <xsl:apply-templates select="out" />
  </table>
</xsl:template>

<xsl:template match="in">
  <tr>
    <th colspan="9">Input</th>
  </tr>
  <xsl:apply-templates select="string | number | boolean | datetime" />
  <xsl:apply-templates select="list" />
  <xsl:apply-templates select="array" />
```

```
  <xsl:apply-templates select="structure" />
  <xsl:apply-templates select="recordset" />
  <xsl:apply-templates select="cookie" />
  <xsl:apply-templates select="file" />
</xsl:template>

<xsl:template match="out">
  <tr>
    <th colspan="9">Output</th>
  </tr>
  <xsl:apply-templates select="string | number | boolean | datetime" />
  <xsl:apply-templates select="list" />
  <xsl:apply-templates select="array" />
  <xsl:apply-templates select="structure" />
  <xsl:apply-templates select="recordset" />
  <xsl:apply-templates select="cookie" />
  <xsl:apply-templates select="file" />
</xsl:template>

<xsl:template match="string">
  <tr>
    <td>Type: string</td>
    <td>Name: <xsl:value-of select="@name" /></td>
    <td>Scope: <xsl:value-of select="@scope" /></td>
    <td>Optional <xsl:value-of select="@optional" /></td>
    <td>Default: <xsl:value-of select="@default" /></td>
    <td>Mask:<xsl:value-of select="@mask" /></td>
    <td>Format:<xsl:value-of select="@format" /></td>
    <td>On Condition:<xsl:value-of select="@oncondition" /></td>
    <td>Comments: <xsl:value-of select="@comments" /></td>
  </tr>
</xsl:template>

<xsl:template match="number">
  <tr>
    <td>Type: number</td>
    <td>Name: <xsl:value-of select="@name" /></td>
    <td>Scope: <xsl:value-of select="@scope" /></td>
    <td>Optional <xsl:value-of select="@optional" /></td>
    <td>Default: <xsl:value-of select="@default" /></td>
    <td>Precision:<xsl:value-of select="@precision" /></td>
    <td>On Condition:<xsl:value-of select="@oncondition" /></td>
    <td colspan="2">Comments: <xsl:value-of select="@comments" /></td>
  </tr>
</xsl:template>

<xsl:template match="boolean">
  <tr>
    <td>Type: boolean</td>
    <td>Name: <xsl:value-of select="@name" /></td>
    <td>Scope: <xsl:value-of select="@scope" /></td>
```

```
    <td>Optional <xsl:value-of select="@optional" /></td>
    <td>Default: <xsl:value-of select="@default" /></td>
    <td>On Condition:<xsl:value-of select="@oncondition" /></td>
    <td colspan="3">Comments: <xsl:value-of select="@comments" /></td>
  </tr>
</xsl:template>
```

```
<xsl:template match="datetime">
  <tr>
    <td>Type: datetime</td>
    <td>Name: <xsl:value-of select="@name" /></td>
    <td>Scope: <xsl:value-of select="@scope" /></td>
    <td>Optional <xsl:value-of select="@optional" /></td>
    <td>Default: <xsl:value-of select="@default" /></td>
    <td>Mask:<xsl:value-of select="@mask" /></td>
    <td>On Condition:<xsl:value-of select="@oncondition" /></td>
    <td colspan="2">Comments: <xsl:value-of select="@comments" /></td>
  </tr>
</xsl:template>

<xsl:template match="list">
  <tr>
    <td colspan="9">
      <table class="listTable">
        <tr>
          <th>Type: List</th>
          <th>Name: <xsl:value-of select="@name" /></th>
          <th>Scope: <xsl:value-of select="@scope" /></th>
          <th>Delimiters: <xsl:value-of select="@delims" /></th>
          <th>Optional: <xsl:value-of select="@optional" /></th>
          <th>Default: <xsl:value-of select="@default" /></th>
          <th>On Condition: <xsl:value-of select="@oncondition" /></th>
          <th>Format: <xsl:value-of select="@format" /></th>
          <th colspan="2">Comments: <xsl:value-of select="@comments" /></th>
        </tr>
      </table>
    </td>
  </tr>
</xsl:template>

<xsl:template match="cookie">
  <tr>
    <td>Type: cookie</td>
    <td>Name: <xsl:value-of select="@name" /></td>
    <td>Expires: <xsl:value-of select="@expires" /></td>
    <td>Secure: <xsl:value-of select="@secure" /></td>
    <td>Format: <xsl:value-of select="@format" /></td>
    <td>Optional <xsl:value-of select="@optional" /></td>
    <td>Default: <xsl:value-of select="@default" /></td>
    <td>On Condition:<xsl:value-of select="@oncondition" /></td>
    <td>Comments: <xsl:value-of select="@comments" /></td>
  </tr>
</xsl:template>

<xsl:template match="file">
  <tr>
    <td>Type: file</td>
    <td colspan="2">Path: <xsl:value-of select="@path" /></td>
```

```
    <td>Action: <xsl:value-of select="@action" /></td>
    <td>Optional <xsl:value-of select="@optional" /></td>
    <td>Default: <xsl:value-of select="@default" /></td>
    <td>On Condition:<xsl:value-of select="@oncondition" /></td>
    <td colspan="2">Comments: <xsl:value-of select="@comments" /></td>
  </tr>
</xsl:template>

<xsl:template match="array">
  <tr>
    <td colspan="9">
      <table class="arrayTable">
        <tr>
          <th>Type: Array</th>
          <th>Name: <xsl:value-of select="@name" /></th>
          <th>Scope: <xsl:value-of select="@scope" /></th>
          <th>Optional: <xsl:value-of select="@optional" /></th>
          <th>On Condition: <xsl:value-of select="@oncondition" /></th>
          <th>Format: <xsl:value-of select="@format" /></th>
          <th colspan="4">Comments: <xsl:value-of select="@comments" /></th>
        </tr>
        <xsl:apply-templates select="string | number | boolean | datetime" />
        <xsl:apply-templates select="array" />
        <xsl:apply-templates select="structure" />
      </table>
    </td>
  </tr>
</xsl:template>

<xsl:template match="structure">
  <tr>
    <td colspan="9">
      <table class="structTable">
        <tr>
          <th>Type: Structure</th>
          <th>Name: <xsl:value-of select="@name" /></th>
          <th>Scope: <xsl:value-of select="@scope" /></th>
          <th>Optional: <xsl:value-of select="@optional" /></th>
          <th>On Condition: <xsl:value-of select="@oncondition" /></th>
          <th>Format: <xsl:value-of select="@format" /></th>
          <th colspan="4">Comments: <xsl:value-of select="@comments" /></th>
        </tr>
        <xsl:apply-templates select="string | number | boolean | datetime" />
        <xsl:apply-templates select="array" />
        <xsl:apply-templates select="structure" />
      </table>
    </td>
  </tr>
</xsl:template>

<xsl:template match="recordset">
```

```
  <tr>
    <td colspan="9">
      <table class="recordsetTable">
        <tr>
          <th>Type: Recordset</th>
          <th>Name: <xsl:value-of select="@name" /></th>
          <th>Primary Keys: <xsl:value-of select="@primarykeys" /></th>
          <th>Scope: <xsl:value-of select="@scope" /></th>
          <th>Optional: <xsl:value-of select="@optional" /></th>
          <th>On Condition: <xsl:value-of select="@oncondition" /></th>
          <th>Format: <xsl:value-of select="@format" /></th>
          <th colspan="2">Comments: <xsl:value-of select="@comments" /></th>
        </tr>
        <xsl:apply-templates select="string | number | boolean | datetime" />
      </table>
    </td>
  </tr>
</xsl:template>

</xsl:stylesheet>
```

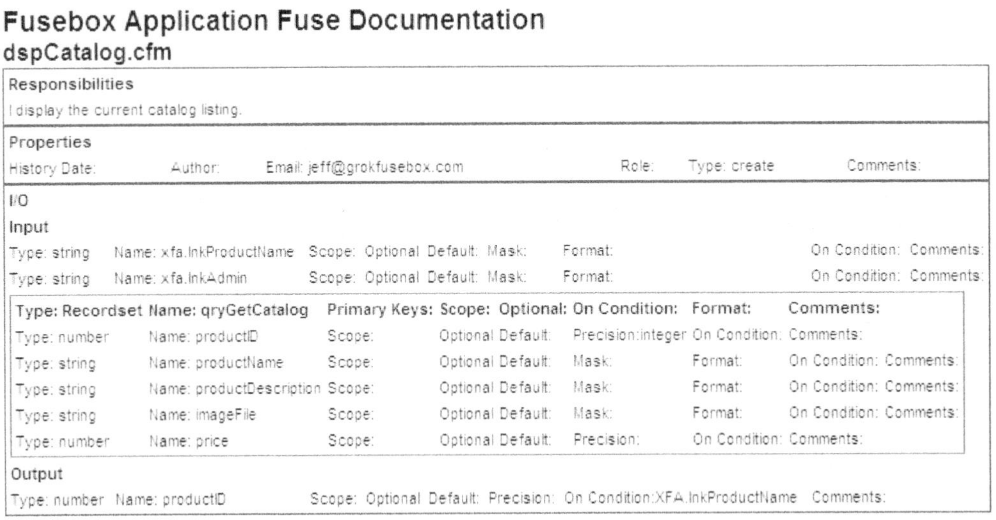

Fusebox Application Fuse Documentation

dspCatalog.cfm

Responsibilities

I display the current catalog listing.

Properties

History Date:	Author:	Email: jeff@grokfusebox.com	Role:	Type: create	Comments:

I/O

Input

Type: string	Name: xfa.lnkProductName	Scope:	Optional	Default:	Mask:	Format:	On Condition:	Comments:
Type: string	Name: xfa.lnkAdmin	Scope:	Optional	Default:	Mask:	Format:	On Condition:	Comments:

Type: Recordset	Name: qryGetCatalog	Primary Keys:	Scope:	Optional:	On Condition:	Format:	Comments:	
Type: number	Name: productID	Scope:	Optional	Default:	Precision:integer	On Condition:	Comments:	
Type: string	Name: productName	Scope:	Optional	Default:	Mask:	Format:	On Condition:	Comments:
Type: string	Name: productDescription	Scope:	Optional	Default:	Mask:	Format:	On Condition:	Comments:
Type: string	Name: imageFile	Scope:	Optional	Default:	Mask:	Format:	On Condition:	Comments:
Type: number	Name: price	Scope:	Optional	Default:	Precision:	On Condition:	Comments:	

Output

Type: number	Name: productID	Scope:	Optional	Default:	Precision:	On Condition:XFA.lnkProductName	Comments:

Illustration 42: FusedocMiner Output for one fuse

Running FusedocMiner with this stylesheet results in a complete book of documentation for a Fusebox 4 application's fuses written to disk, and a progress/error report written to the browser, as seen in Illustration 43. This report lets us know when there are any problems with the XML in a given Fusedoc. The power is right at our fingertips.

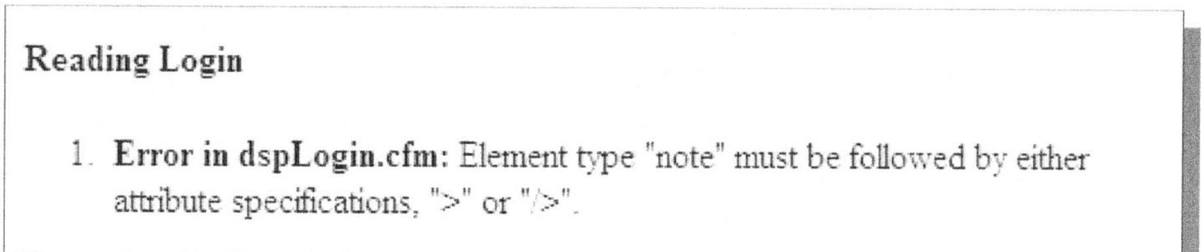

Reading Login

1. **Error in dspLogin.cfm:** Element type "note" must be followed by either attribute specifications, ">" or "/>".

Illustration 43: FusedocMiner Error Output

Chapter 9 - It All Comes Together

We've managed to get through an entire book on using XML in CFML. I hope you're feeling very encouraged by the information contained here, and ready to go out and build awesome XML-based "stuff" of your own. It's really pretty easy when you get down and take a look at it, isn't it?

So what have we been through in this book? Let's take a quick recap:

- In Chapter 01 - Introduction to XML, we took a look at what XML is and why it's important in today's application environment.

- In Chapter 02 - XML Objects in CFML, we explored the difference between XML data in string form and XML objects (documents) in CFML.

- In Chapter 03 - Creating XML Objects, we learned how to create CFML XML objects using a variety of methods, including the <CFXML> tag and the XmlParse() function.

- In Chapter 04 - Output from XML Objects, we used XSLT transformations and the tostring() function to output XML data in forms we want.

- In Chapter 05 - Getting Data from XML Objects, we used the XmlSearch() function and XPath to extract specific pieces of data from XML datasets.

- In Chapter 06 - XML Functions in CFML, we took a closer look at other functions that are available for manipulating XML in CFML.

- In Chapter 07 – WDDX, we used Web Distributed Data Exchange to move data between disparate environments like CFML and Javascript.

- In Chapter 08 - XML and Fusebox, we took a practical look at how XML can provide a whole set of useful tools for managing and documenting Fusebox 4 development projects.

- And now in Chapter 9 we're wrapping it all up.

There is additional information available in the Appendices as well—just some quick reference material to make finding the goods a bit quicker.

It is my genuine hope that this book gives you a great deal more value in return than you paid for it. I'm always eager to hear from readers, especially if you have ideas about how to improve future volumes. Drop me a line anytime at jeff@grokfusebox.com

Now on with your XML!

Appendix A – The CFXML Tag

The <CFXML> tag is used to convert XML data in text format into a CFML XML object.

Syntax:

```
<cfxml variable="foo" [casesensitive="false|true"]>
  <well-formed-xml-code-here />
</cfxml>
```

Attributes:

variable (string): the name of the XML object variable to create.

casesensitive (boolean): whether to treat the enclosed XML code strictly in terms of case, e.g. if True, **`myName`** is not the same as **`myname`**. Default is True.

Example:

```
<cfxml variable="foo">
  <myTeam>
    <person name="Vic" />
    <person name="Lisa" />
  </myTeam>
</cfxml>
```

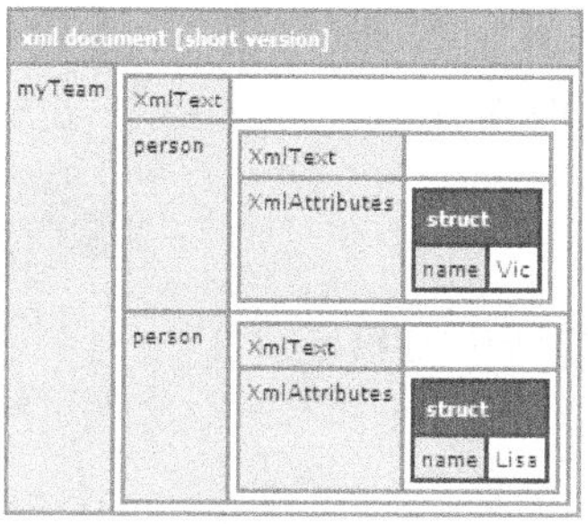

Illustration 44: <CFXML> Example Result

Appendix B – XML Functions

NOTE: All examples in this appendix are given in CFScript syntax.

IsWDDX()

Returns True if stringArgument is a WDDX-compliant XML dataset; otherwise returns False.

Syntax:

```
return = IsWDDX(stringArgument)
```

Example:

```
<cfscript>
  myArray = ArrayNew(1);
  myArray[1] = "Ace";
  myArray[2] = "Deuce";
</cfscript>
<cfwddx action="cfml2wddx" input="#myArray#" output="myWDDXPacket">
<cfdump var="#IsWDDX(myWDDXPacket)#">
```

IsXML()

Returns True if stringArgument is an XML-compliant dataset; otherwise returns False.

Syntax:

```
return = IsXML(stringArgument)
```

Example:

```
<cfscript>
 strXML = '';
 strXML = '#strXML#<team name="Bluejays">';
 strXML = '#strXML# <person name="John" />';
 strXML = '#strXML# <person name="Jane" />';
 strXML = '#strXML#</team>';
</cfscript>

<cfdump var="#IsXML(strXML)#">
<cfdump var="#strXML#">
```

NOTE: IsXML() does not exist in BlueDragon 6.x

IsXmlAttribute()

Returns True if nodeArgument is an attribute node within an XML object; otherwise returns False.

Syntax:

```
return = IsXmlAttribute(nodeArgument)
```

Note: nodeArgument values are typically retrieved using XmlSearch().

Example:

```
<cfscript>
 strXML = '';
 strXML = '#strXML#<team name="Bluejays">';
 strXML = '#strXML# <person name="John" />';
 strXML = '#strXML# <person name="Jane" />';
 strXML = '#strXML#</team>';
 xmlTeam = XmlParse(strXML);
 teamName = XmlSearch(xmlTeam,'/team/@name');
</cfscript>

<cfdump var="#IsXMLAttribute(teamName)#">
```

Note: IsXmlAttribute() does not exist in BlueDragon 6.x.

IsXmlDoc()

Returns True if variable is a CFML XML object (document); otherwise returns False.

Syntax:

```
return = IsXMLDoc(variable)
```

Example:

```
<cfscript>
  strXML = '';
  strXML = '#strXML#<team name="Bluejays">';
  strXML = '#strXML# <person name="John" />';
  strXML = '#strXML# <person name="Jane" />';
  strXML = '#strXML#</team>';
  xmlTeam = XmlParse(strXML);
</cfscript>

<cfdump var="#IsXMLDoc(xmlTeam)#">
```

IsXmlElem()

Returns True if nodeArgument is an element node within an XML object; otherwise returns False.

Syntax:

```
return = IsXmlElem(nodeArgument)
```

Note: nodeArgument values are typically retrieved using XmlSearch().

Sample:

```
<cfscript>
  strXML = '';
  strXML = '#strXML#<team name="Bluejays">';
  strXML = '#strXML# <person name="John" />';
  strXML = '#strXML# <person name="Jane" />';
  strXML = '#strXML#</team>';
  teamNode = XmlSearch(strXML,'/team');
</cfscript>

<cfdump var="#IsXMLElem(teamNode)#">
```

IsXmlNode()

Returns True if nodeArgument is a node within an XML object; otherwise returns False.

Syntax:

```
return = IsXmlNode(nodeArgument)
```

Note: nodeArgument values are typically retrieved using XmlSearch().

Sample:

```
<cfscript>
 strXML = '';
 strXML = '#strXML#<team name="Bluejays">';
 strXML = '#strXML# <person name="John" />';
 strXML = '#strXML# <person name="Jane" />';
 strXML = '#strXML#</team>';
 teamNode = XmlSearch(strXML,'/team');
</cfscript>

<cfdump var="#IsXMLNode(teamNode)#">
```

Note: IsXmlNode() does not exist in BlueDragon 6.x.

IsXmlRoot()

Returns True if nodeArgument is the root element within an XML object; otherwise returns False.

Syntax:

```
return = IsXmlRoot(nodeArgument)
```

Example:

```
<cfscript>
  strXML = '';
  strXML = '#strXML#<team name="Bluejays">';
  strXML = '#strXML# <person name="John" />';
  strXML = '#strXML# <person name="Jane" />';
  strXML = '#strXML#</team>';
  xmlTeam = XmlParse(strXML);
</cfscript>

<cfdump var='#IsXmlRoot(xmlTeam.team)#'>
```

ToString()

Returns an XML string representation of a CFML XML object's data, prepending the XML document declaration <?xml version="1.0" encoding="UTF-8"?>. The tostring() function is a built-in method of a CFML XML object. It takes no arguments.

Syntax:

```
return = tostring(myXmlDoc)
```

Example:

```
<cfscript>
 strXML = '';
 strXML = '#strXML#<team name="Bluejays">';
 strXML = '#strXML# <person name="John" />';
 strXML = '#strXML# <person name="Jane" />';
 strXML = '#strXML#</team>';
 xmlTeam = XmlParse(strXML);
</cfscript>

<cfoutput>
 #HTMLCodeFormat(tostring(xmlTeam))#
</cfoutput>
```

BlueDragon also implements tostring() as a method of the XML document object. So the following example is valid for BlueDragon:

```
<cfscript>
 strXML = '';
 strXML = '#strXML#<team name="Bluejays">';
 strXML = '#strXML# <person name="John" />';
 strXML = '#strXML# <person name="Jane" />';
 strXML = '#strXML#</team>';
 xmlTeam = XmlParse(strXML);
</cfscript>

<cfoutput>
 #HTMLCodeFormat(xmlTeam.tostring())#
</cfoutput>
```

XmlChildPos()

Returns the position of the nth iteration of childNodeName with the parentElement's childNodes array. In the example, the first iteration of a **`mascot`** child is the third overall child node of the **`<team>`** element.

Syntax:

```
whichChild = XmlChildPos(parentElement, childNodeName,n)
```

Example:

```
<cfscript>
  strXML = '';
  strXML = '#strXML#<team name="Bluejays">';
  strXML = '#strXML# <person name="John" />';
  strXML = '#strXML# <person name="Jane" />';
  strXML = '#strXML# <mascot name="Streak" type="bird" />';
  strXML = '#strXML#</team>';
  xmlTeam = XmlParse(strXML);
  mascotSlot = XmlChildPos(xmlTeam.team,"mascot",1);
</cfscript>

<cfdump var="#mascotSlot#">
```

XmlElemNew()

Returns a new XML elementName element in the namespace namespaceAttribute. Used to construct XML objects. If no namespace is desired, namespaceAttribute should be the XML object where the new node is being created.

Syntax:

```
newElement = XmlElemNew(namespaceAttribute,elementName);
```

Example:

```
<cfscript>
 xmlTeam = XmlNew();
 xmlTeam.xmlRoot = XmlElemNew(xmlTeam,"team");
 xmlTeam.team.XmlAttributes.name = "Bluejays";
 xmlTeam.team.XmlChildren[1] = XmlElemNew(xmlTeam,"person");
 xmlTeam.team.person[1].XmlAttributes.name = "John";
 xmlTeam.team.XmlChildren[2] = XmlElemNew(xmlTeam,"person");
 xmlTeam.team.person[2].XmlAttributes.name = "Jane";
 xmlTeam.team.XmlChildren[3] = XmlElemNew(xmlTeam,"mascot");
 xmlTeam.team.mascot.XmlAttributes.name = "Streak";
 xmlTeam.team.mascot.XmlAttributes.type = "bird";
</cfscript>

<cfdump var="#xmlTeam#">
```

XmlFormat()

Returns argumentString in XML-compliant form. The result can be used in XML datasets and objects (usually in the XmlText of an XML object).

Syntax:

```
return = XmlFormat(argumentString);
```

Example:

```
<cfset myString = XmlFormat("Martin & Lewis <great>; Laurel & Hardy <okay>")>

<cfoutput>
 #HTMLCodeFormat(myString)#
</cfoutput>
```

XmlGetNodeType()

Returns the the XML node type of the nodeArgument.

Syntax:

```
return = XmlGetNodeType(nodeArgument)
```

Example:

```
<cfscript>
  strXML = '';
  strXML = '#strXML#<team name="Bluejays">';
  strXML = '#strXML# <person name="John" />';
  strXML = '#strXML# <person name="Jane" />';
  strXML = '#strXML# <mascot name="Streak" type="eagle" />';
  strXML = '#strXML#</team>';
  xmlTeam = XmlParse(strXML);
</cfscript>

<cfloop from="1" to="#ArrayLen(xmlTeam.team.xmlNodes)#" index="i">
  <cfoutput>#XmlGetNodeType(xmlTeam.team.xmlNodes[i])#</cfoutput>
</cfloop>
```

Note: XmlGetNodeType() does not exist in BlueDragon 6.x.

XmlNew()

Returns a new, empty CFML XML object.

Syntax:

```
newElement = XmlNew();
```

Example:

```
<cfscript>
  xmlTeam = XmlNew();
  xmlTeam.xmlRoot = XmlElemNew(xmlTeam,"team");
  xmlTeam.team.XmlAttributes.name = "Bluejays";
  xmlTeam.team.XmlChildren[1] = XmlElemNew(xmlTeam,"person");
  xmlTeam.team.person[1].XmlAttributes.name = "John";
  xmlTeam.team.XmlChildren[2] = XmlElemNew(xmlTeam,"person");
  xmlTeam.team.person[2].XmlAttributes.name = "Jane";
  xmlTeam.team.XmlChildren[3] = XmlElemNew(xmlTeam,"mascot");
  xmlTeam.team.mascot.XmlAttributes.name = "Streak";
  xmlTeam.team.mascot.XmlAttributes.type = "bird";
</cfscript>

<cfdump var="#xmlTeam#">
```

XmlParse()

Parses xmlDataString and returns a CFML XML object. The single argument must be a string representing a well-formed XML dataset.

Syntax:

```
xmlObj = XmlParse(xmlDataString);
```

Example:

```
<cfscript>
 strXML = '';
 strXML = '#strXML#<team name="Bluejays">';
 strXML = '#strXML# <person name="John" />';
 strXML = '#strXML# <person name="Jane" />';
 strXML = '#strXML# <mascot name="Streak" type="eagle" />';
 strXML = '#strXML#</team>';
 xmlTeam = XmlParse(strXML);
</cfscript>

<cfdump var="#xmlTeam#">
```

XmlSearch()

Returns results from xmlObj that match the specification in xpathSearchString. The first argument (xmlObj) must be a CFML XML object, and the second argument (xpathSearchString) must be a valid XPath search string.

Syntax:

```
result = XmlSearch(xmlObj,xpathSearchString);
```

Example:

```
<cfscript>
 strXML = '';
 strXML = '#strXML#<team name="Bluejays">';
 strXML = '#strXML# <person name="John" />';
 strXML = '#strXML# <person name="Jane" />';
 strXML = '#strXML# <mascot name="Streak" type="eagle" />';
 strXML = '#strXML#</team>';
 xmlTeam = XmlParse(strXML);
 result = XmlSearch(xmlTeam,"/team/person[@name='John']");
</cfscript>

<cfdump var="#result#">
```

XmlTransform()

Returns the result of an XSL transformation by applying the XSL code in xslString to the XML data in xmlString. Returns an error if either input is not well-formed.

Syntax:

```
return = XmlTransform(xmlString,xslString);
```

Example:

```
<cfscript>
 strXML = '<team name="Bluejays">';
 strXML = '#strXML# <person name="John" />';
 strXML = '#strXML# <person name="Jane" />';
 strXML = '#strXML# <mascot name="Streak" type="eagle" />';
 strXML = '#strXML#</team>';
 strXSL = '<?xml version="1.0"?>';
 strXSL = '#strXSL#<xsl:stylesheet version="1.0" xmlns:xsl="http://www.w3.org/1999/XSL/Transform">';
 strXSL = '#strXSL#<xsl:output method="html" doctype-public="-//W3C//DTD HTML 4.0 Transitional//EN" />';
 strXSL = '#strXSL#<xsl:template match="/">';
 strXSL = '#strXSL#  <html><head><title>My Team</title></head>';
 strXSL = '#strXSL#    <body>'<xsl:apply-templates select="team" /></body>';
 strXSL = '#strXSL#  </html>';
 strXSL = '#strXSL#</xsl:template>';
 strXSL = '#strXSL#<xsl:template match="team">';
 strXSL = '#strXSL#  <table border="1" align="center" width="400">';
 strXSL = '#strXSL#    <xsl:apply-templates select="person" />';
 strXSL = '#strXSL#  </table>';
 strXSL = '#strXSL#</xsl:template>';
 strXSL = '#strXSL#<xsl:template match="person">';
 strXSL = '#strXSL#  <tr><td>';
 strXSL = '#strXSL#    <xsl:value-of select="@name" />';
 strXSL = '#strXSL#  </td></tr>';
 strXSL = '#strXSL#</xsl:template>';
 strXSL = '#strXSL#</xsl:stylesheet>';
 result = XmlTransform(strXML,strXSL);
</cfscript>
<cfoutput>#result#</cfoutput>
```

Note: This example is atypical. XML and XSL data will normally be read from outside sources such as disk files, web services, etc.

XmlValidate()

Returns a structure of data with information about the validity of xmlData as validated against schemaOrDTD. The first parameter (xmlData) may reference an XML dataset in any of several ways. It can be an XML data string, the name of a local file that contains XML data, a URL that returns an XML dataset, or a CFML XML object (as created by XmlParse() or <CFXML>). The second parameter (schemaOrDTD) may reference a schema or DTD in the same ways, except for the last (CFML XML object). URLs may point to http, https, ftp, or file resources.

If the validation is successful, **`result.status`** will be YES; otherwise it will be NO (assuming the return is assigned to the variable **`result`**).

Syntax:

```
result = XmlValidate(xmlData,schemaOrDTD);
```

Example:

```
<cfscript>
 strXML = '';
 strXML = '#strXML#<circuit access="public">';
 strXML = '#strXML# <fuseaction name="showCatalog">';
 strXML = '#strXML#     <xfa name="lnkProductName" value="browse.showProduct" />';
 strXML = '#strXML#     <xfa name="lnkAdmin" value="Admin.showNewProductForm" />';
 strXML = '#strXML#     <include template="qryGetCatalog" />';
 strXML = '#strXML#     <include template="dspCatalog"/>';
 strXML = '#strXML# </fuseaction>';
 strXML = '#strXML# <fuseaction name="showProduct">';
 strXML = '#strXML#   <xfa name="lnkBackToCatalog" value="browse.showCatalog" />';
 strXML = '#strXML#   <include template="qryGetProduct" />';
 strXML = '#strXML#     <include template="dspProduct" />';
 strXML = '#strXML# </fuseaction>';
 strXML = '#strXML#</circuit>';

 result = XmlValidate(strXML,"http://localhost/fusebox/circuit.dtd");
</cfscript>

<cfdump var="#result#">
```

Note: XmlValidate() does not exist in BlueDragon 6.x

Appendix C – XPath Expressions

XPath provides a means of returning specific data from an XML dataset. Expressions can be constructed to identify elements according to their names, their attributes, and their membership in various groups.

Elements

Elements are represented in XML as tags. XPath can return individual elements or groups of elements, depending on the syntax of the XPath expression.

XPath Syntax	Interpretation
elementname	All child nodes of the element
/	Expression is relative to the dataset's root element
//	Expression selects all descendants (of the node to the left of the //) that match the expression.
.	Matches the current element's parent

XPath Syntax	Interpretation
..	Matches the current element's parent
@attributename	Matches the named attribute

Predicates

Predicates are a means of narrowing an XPath search. They provide the ability to identify specific elements according to data in the elements' attributes, or the elements' membership in special groups called axes. Predicates are indicated by square brackets [].

XPath Syntax	Interpretation
elementname[n]	Returns the nth elementname element
elementname[last()]	Returns the last elementname element
elementname[last()-n]	Returns the elementname element that is n positions from last
elementname[position()>n]	Returns all elementname elements that are after the nth elementname element
elementname[@attributename]	Returns elementname elements that have an attribute named attributename
elementname[@attributename='value']	Returns elementname elements that have an attribute named attributename equal to value.
element1[element2=value]	Returns element1 elements that have children of element2 with a value of value. (element2 is an element, NOT an attribute)

Operators

The following operators are available for use in XPath predicates and axes.

XPath Operator	Interpretation
|	Result contains both node sets
+	Addition
*	Multiplication
div	Division
=	Equal to
!=	Not equal to
<	Less than
<=	Less than or equal to
>	Greater than
>=	Greater than or equal to
or	Logical OR
and	Logical AND
mod	Modulo (remainder after division)

Attributes

Attributes are represented in XML as name-value pairs within an element's starting tag.

The important thing to recognize about attributes is that we can use them in a couple of different ways when designing XPath queries. First, as shown in the Element section above, we can return an actual attribute node, using the syntax @attributename. So /vehicles/vehicle/@hatchback would return the hatchback attribute of the vehicle element. Second, as shown in the Predicates section above, we can use attributes as selection criteria for elements, using the syntaxes [@attributename] or [@attributename operator value]. So /vehicles/vehicle[@hatchback] would return vehicle elements with a hatchback attribute, and /vehicles/vehicle[@hatchback='yes'] would return vehicle elements with a hatchback attribute set to **yes**.

Axes

Axes are a special notation in XPath syntax for returning collections or groups of nodes.

Axis	Interpretation
ancestor	Returns all ancestors (parent, grandparent, etc.) of the current node
ancestor-or-self	Returns all ancestors (parent, grandparent, etc.) of the current node plus the current node
attribute	Returns all attributes of the current node
child	Returns all children of the current node
descendant	Returns all descendants (children, grandchildren, etc.) of the current node
descendant-or-self	Returns all descendants (children, grandchildren, etc.) of the current node plus the current node
following	Returns all nodes in the dataset after the current

Axis	Interpretation
	node
following-sibling	Returns all siblings (same level) after the current node
parent	Returns the parent of the current node
preceding	Returns everything in the dataset that is before the current node
preceding-sibling	Returns all siblings (same level) before the current node
self	Returns the current node

Axes can be modified with two colons followed by further specifications. For example, child::element1 would return all the element1 children of the current element.

Alphabetical Index

Illustration Index

Made in the USA
Monee, IL
08 November 2026

68020212R00092